THE
Journey
TO *Joy*

THE Journey TO Joy

5 Generations Share Stories
Every Woman Needs to Hear

JOY FITZGERALD
WITH SA PHILLIPS & TAYLOR FITZGERALD

MYND
MATTERS

Mynd Matters Publishing
201 17th Street NW, Suite 300, Atlanta, GA 30363
www.myndmatterspublishing.com

Library of Congress Control Number: 2018911104
ISBN-13: 978-1-948145-15-2

FIRST EDITION

Printed in the United States of America

To Charity Maples, the matriarch of our family. You have taught me how to love, laugh, and be a strong woman.

A SPECIAL THANKS

Writing a book is a journey in and of itself. This collection of stories was compiled and published in honor of my great-grandmother, Charity Maples, and the five generations of strong women in my family. Throughout the process, I gained a deeper love and respect for the women who shared their experiences and wisdom throughout these pages. To our surprise, we each learned a story about one another that we did not know prior to writing the book. This brought us closer and we grew to value our strength even more.

These stories represent some of the private and personal moments throughout our journey as women. While there have been many amazing moments and happy times in our lives, we've all experienced hardships, pain, and heartbreak. Although the downsides of life are not unique to us, we have learned that with a strong network of women, wise counsel, faith and love, JOY does come in the morning.

I would like to first thank God as I am blessed through my direct lineage to have five generations of women living, as my daughter was the first to begin the fifth generation.

I would like to thank my great-grandmother for sharing her wisdom, derived from 100 years of life experiences, and testimonies of faith. Thanks to my grandmother, Ruth, for countless hours spent on the phone reliving a lifetime of memories. For both, revisiting these stories was not always easy, but they shared their truths in a vulnerable and transparent way to help each of us learn and grow.

To my dream builder: Mom, you served as the wind beneath my wings in encouraging and activating this vision. You have selflessly given your time, skills, and ideas without any expectation other than making my dream come true. Thank you for allowing me to be vulnerable, have moments of doubt, call all times of the night with new ideas, and most importantly, for believing in me. With every phone call, you inspired and encouraged me to imagine an even bigger future.

To my dream advisor: Taylor, you have been my greatest advisor and consultant. You challenged me to think differently and expand the view in which I see things. You were my voice of reason who I called on to test new ideas and guide me in the right direction. Throughout this process, you served as the boss that I didn't always ask for, but certainly needed.

It is because of the both of you, this lifelong dream of writing a book is now a reality.

To my husband Tyron: thanks for being my strongest supporter and biggest cheerleader. You are my rock. You encourage me to be better and not let anyone or anything stand in my way. You gave me the best gift in December when you asked this heart piercing question, "What can I take off your plate to allow you the time and focus you need to write your book? Whatever it is, give it to me and I will take it." Wow! I still tear up every time I reflect on that conversation.

Baby, you embody everything that I could ever want in a husband and because of your support and resources, we did it!

To my son Tyron Jr. (aka Jessie): thanks for being my protector. You were the silent voice that made sure that I balanced my time. Thanks for coming into the office late at night when everyone else was asleep to say, "Mom, I think it's time you stop writing and get some sleep." Thanks for sharing me with this book as I know it required you to give up some of our quality time. You are a source of inspiration.

To my dad Melvin: thanks for being the unassigned proofreader. You have read more stories than anyone in the family. It is because you cared and wanted to be involved in the project in whatever way that you could. In my mind, that's priceless.

To my sister Kristy: thanks for being a counselor and strategist in thinking through the big picture. You gave great ideas and challenged me to write stories that I may not have written.

To my wonderful team: Janice Chavers, my proofreader, thanks for your encouragement and advice. Johnathon Givens, who is the best graphic designer, and website guru - you rock. Thanks to Renita Bryant and the great team at Mynd Matters Publishing for believing in the project and helping to usher me through the journey of publishing.

To my book club members and my girlfriends: thanks for the support and encouragement to pursue this dream. I also want to thank Angela Roberts for being a strong supporter and thought partner throughout the entire process.

To my mentors and author friends: Lisa Nichols and Dr. Sharon Melnick, thanks for your advice and push to put the plan into action.

CONTENTS

Introduction
YOU ARE NOT ALONE

Thank you for purchasing this book. Your decision may have been based upon the title, a recommendation from a friend, or maybe you chose to take a chance on a random selection. Whatever your reason, you have purpose in exploring the words and ideas between the following pages.

Perhaps you're on a journey to discovering who you are, feeling alone, or not fully understanding your purpose in life. This book is a "walk along," profoundly rooted journey of real stories filled with passion, encompassing a wide variety of life-learned lessons and experiences. It's a true saying *that experience is the best teacher.*

For years, I have served as a catalyst in encouraging people to push boundaries and own their development to reach their life goals. During my journey, I have heard stories of depression, pain, and brokenness. Many have shared feelings of confusion on how to navigate successfully in roles such as being a mother, wife, daughter-in-law, grandmother, career professional, and the list goes on. Ultimately, everyone is on a journey to finding more love, peace, hope, and ultimately, joy.

As I coach women, I find that many are on a quest that at times feels like a hopeless, never-ending road. They search but quickly recognize that life has presented what often appears to be insurmountable challenges.

What should they do and where should they go? They are pillars of strength within their families so what would people think if they knew the pillar is on the verge of crumbling? It' a vulnerable place that women rarely want to visit.

I hear stories of loss, bad relationships with men, crazy stories with men, hopeless stories with men, lazy men, unfaithful men, and yes, good men. The women cry over health issues, including painful menstrual cycles, miscarriages, body changes, infertility, menopause, stretch marks, and many other specifics that tend to go hand-in-hand with life as a woman. They wonder what they should do and if what they experience is "normal."

But long before they were women with questions, they were girls with dreams. Now, these girls are growing up and facing their own evolution of self-esteem, self-love, and self-discovery. Although they want to be happy, they lack the confidence and advice needed to navigate life's journey. And yes, it's a journey. Unfortunately, some become complacent within the confines of where they are and what they have and give up on where they desire to be. Leading to being unfulfilled with regrets and minimal purpose.

These are the stories of countless women as they struggle to understand the complexities of being a woman in various stages of life. Only a few have mothers, grandmothers, or great-grandmothers in their lives to seek counsel when they face life's struggles. Thankfully, I am blessed to have over 100 combined years of on-demand, female advice living in my family.

Spanning across five generations, from twenty-two to the oldest at 100 years of age, we have witnessed the lows of the Great Depression, the highs of the Civil Rights Movement, and the progression of modern years. Our experiences are varied and our words made plain between the following pages. Just as I've been inspired by the countless women I have encountered, I am encouraged by the stories we share. This book was written for you and the courageous men who want to understand you.

The Journey to Joy shares untold stories every woman needs to hear. Each generation offers a unique perspective on raw and real topics offering truths few want to discuss. We are open, honest, and most of all, vulnerable. We expose the sacred places of our hearts to help you in your journey of finding and keeping more joy. We share stories of faith, courage, grief, hardship, and strength. Each includes a lesson and reflection questions. To get the most out of *The Journey to Joy*, be sure to use the companion guided journal, *The Journal to Joy*. It is essential that you take time to reflect on each story and acknowledge your thoughts, feelings, and truths. The stories will make you laugh, cry, grow, reflect, and better understand that you are not alone.

We invite you into our family's living room while we share our experiences so that you too can hear from a daughter, mother, grandmother, great-grandmother, and great-great-grandmother. Think of it as wholesome reality TV in book form. If your loved ones are no longer alive, or if you are seeking wisdom from a different perspective, explore these words and find the love, support, and direction that you may be missing.

Also, we don't leave out the men. It is for you too! We are hopeful that each reader will better understand the power and strength of being a woman and how to love the women in their life better so that they can experience real JOY.

FIVE GENERATIONS OF STRENGTH

First Generation: Charity Maples

Who are you? I am Charity Louisiana King Maples, the daughter of Monroe King and Margaret Morgan. I was born on June 4, 1918. I am 100 years old. I was married to Perry Maples and together we had eight beautiful children. I have survived being a widow at the age of thirty-three along with the death of my parents, two children, and all my brothers and sisters. I have endured birthing eight children without the aid of doctors or a hospital, living in poverty, the hardships of racism, and the lack of food and clothing. However, through it all, I have found great joy. I have never had one surgery and consider myself as having lived a blessed life. I have dedicated my entire life to the church and serving God.

Name something unique about you. I have a photographic memory. I can remember things as early as one and a half years of age. I remember every story, poem, or song that I have read. Even at the ripe age of 100, I can recall those things as if they happened yesterday. How many can say they remember the first thing they ever read? I can. I believe that if I had been born in a different generation, I would have been someone great. I would have had an opportunity to use my mind in ways that weren't accessible to Black women back then. I sometimes think I could've been a computer like the women in that movie, *Hidden Figures*.

What is your most significant accomplishment? Raising my children with the love and fear of God. I love children and my children have brought me great joy.

What is your favorite story in the book and why? *Kingdom Fruit.* It shares my love and prayer for children. It speaks to my heart's desire to serve the world and God's kingdom.

What is the legacy you want to leave in the world? Years from now, I want my next generations to know that I was an ordinary woman that loved children. I want them to be obedient to their parents and teach their children how to take care of themselves. It is important to teach children how to love and be kind to others. Grow up and be happy. In essence, I want to leave the gift of how to love and raise children for my next generations, because the children are our future. If we don't get this right, we won't have a world to leave anything to.

Second Generation: Ruth Givens

Who are you? My name is Ruth Givens and I am eighty-years old. My husband and I were married for over fifty years until he died. Sewing is one of my favorite hobbies. I can make anything from clothes to window treatments. I also love teaching as I have been a Sunday School teacher for over forty years. I am in great health and I have never had a surgery in my life. I still drive my car, live alone, and can do anything anyone else can. I am a passionate and sensitive person. People who know me best would say that I am serious as I have always been mature for my age.

Name something unique about you. I am a forgiving person. I believe this is a unique value and personality trait that the world needs. Honestly, you can't love if you can't forgive.

What is your greatest accomplishment? Raising my children. When God blesses you with children, they are miracle gifts. They should be cherished and handled with care. Parents should raise them in a special way that God would be pleased because they are created in His image and likeness. All of my children are in the church. No drugs, jail, alcohol, nor divorces. This is my greatest accomplishment.

What is your favorite story in the book and why? *My Little Became Much.* This is the story that I am still living, even at eighty. I have always lived in faith and believed the scripture in the Bible that states, "I have been young, and *now* am old; yet have I not seen the righteous forsaken, nor his seed begging bread." (Psalm 37:25 KJV) God promised that He would never leave us nor forsake us. God is keeping me and making sure all of my needs are being met. In this story, I share how my little has always been much.

What is the legacy you want to leave in the world? I want people to know that I am a woman of my word. If I tell you I am going to do something, you can count on it. I practice being punctual and I detest being late. Mostly, I want to instill in the world the confidence to know that if anyone else can do it, you can too! Don't let anyone tell you otherwise.

Third Generation: Ann Phillips

Who are you? I am Shirley Ann Phillips, a new age woman in my early sixties. I never really liked the name Shirley because there were two other relatives with the same name. As most true southern folks do, they referred to Shirley Ann #1 as Big Shirley, and Shirley Ann #2 as Shirlann. Need I say anymore? Early in my teen years, I dropped the name Shirley and became known only as Ann.

I'm a wife, mother, and a Nana. I'm an original (which is why I dropped the name Shirley) and an individualist; someone not afraid to stand alone, stand out, or speak up for right causes when others won't. I'm a jack of all trades and a master of some. I'm a musician, a licensed realtor, a seamstress, a golfer, and I have a small in-home business. I'm never bored because I love working with my hands and have a wide array of interests. My problem is that I don't have enough time, or the stamina, to do all the things that I desire.

Name Something Unique About You. I love coloring books. I've been coloring long before it became a popular "adult" thing to do. I still possess coloring books that were my children's when they were small and have recycled those same books and colored in them with my grandchildren. Oh, and I love talk radio and especially sports talk shows.

What Is Your Greatest Accomplishment? One of my greatest accomplishments was going to college at a late stage in my life. I went to night school on weekends and took online classes for eight years, which was not easy and somewhat humbling to be in school with students young enough to be my children. In fact, at one point my oldest daughter and I were in school at the same time but I persevered!

What is your favorite story in the book and why? I like them all! I feel a sense of ownership because this was a collaborative effort in giving voice to pain, turmoil, happiness, grief, uncertainty, passion, and sharing them in the form of stories on paper.

What is the legacy you want to leave in the world? I don't want my living to be in vain. I don't want to be someone who just occupied a space for a period of years with no value or worth. My legacy is my children and my grandchildren. I am still investing in them the best of what I know, what I have learned, and who I am so that they can take it a little farther and make it better!

Fourth Generation: Joy Fitzgerald

Who are you? I am a mother, daughter, wife, friend, Chief Diversity Officer, speaker, life coach, and author. I have spent over twenty-five years in corporate America designing human capital solutions that drive peak performance. But basically, I am a little girl that grew up in Memphis, Tennessee who always had a desire to heal the world and help people. I am an agent of change who desires to speak more love and joy into the hearts and minds of everyone I am blessed and honored to meet. People who know me best would say I am the perfect articulation of my name, JOY.

Name something unique about you. My God-given ability to influence and change the hearts and minds of people. Throughout my professional career, I have often been faced with the challenge of influencing others. In my two roles as Chief Diversity Officer, this has been a more significant challenge. In relatively short amounts of time, I have been successful in moving the hearts and minds of people with very strong beliefs that have been resistant to change. I am not afraid to speak truth to power, especially when I believe in something.

What is your most significant accomplishment? Raising my children. Admittedly, my children are a weak spot for me. My joy as a mother is the one role at which I never want to fail. Being a mother is a sacred gift and I treasure my children's opinions. I strive to be a great example and role model and have dedicated my life and made many sacrifices for them. I continue to pour every piece of love, wisdom, encouragement, affection, and joy into my children. I am proud of who they are and I can't wait to see all that they will accomplish.

What is your favorite story in the book and why? *Miscarriages and Angels in the Sky* as it shares my struggle with loss and the fear of infertility. I reveal the insecurities I faced in having a child. I am prayerful that my vulnerability will provide encouragement and hope for many women facing a similar situation.

What is the legacy you want to leave in the world? I want to share and speak joy into the world. I genuinely believe that this is my purpose and divine assignment in life. It is my hope and prayer that God will honor my service and allow me to impart his love into the world.

Fifth Generation:
Taylor Fitzgerald

Who are you? I am a twenty-two-year-old young lady that is living her *best* life. In May 2018, I graduated from Indiana University and am currently a pharmaceutical sales representative at a Fortune 200 company. I recently relocated to Memphis, Tennessee after living in three different states in the last five years. On most days, I enjoy arts and crafts and have a natural talent for making and building things. I am most excited when beginning a new project. I am a woman of strong faith and moral principles. Hence, I choose friends very carefully as it is important to surround myself with individuals who have the same values that I do. People who know me best call me an "old soul." I am totally okay with this articulation as it represents my fervent commitment and deep rooting in family values.

Name something unique about you. I consider myself a divergent or possibly, a generalist. I am not limited to one particular strength or area of focus as I am interested in many different things. Unapologetically, I am talented in varying areas, which has made life unusual as I don't have any one thing that I cannot do. Over time, I have grown to see my comprehensive list of talents as a unique strength.

What is your most significant accomplishment? Learning to love myself. As a young girl, and even now, my mom has been my role model. She is beautiful, successful, and very petite. She is a little under five feet and weighs less than 120 pounds. Imagine growing up bigger and taller than your mom. It was a struggle because like most girls, I wanted to share clothes and shoes with her but that was not our reality. I had to learn to love me, including my body, shape, size, skin, and all of the traits that were unique in defining me. Once I did, I began to live a joyful life. Of all the people you will love across a lifetime, the most important is the love you have for yourself. *Learn to love you!*

What is your favorite story in the book and why? *Doubt* because it shares one of the greatest stages in finding my journey to joy. It is extremely personal and highlights many of the insecurities I faced growing up. I shared this experience to encourage and empower other girls and women to face, confront, and overcome doubt.

What is the legacy you want to leave in the world? I can comfortably admit that I don't have an answer. That response alone is part of my growth, journey, and maturity. In the past, I would have made up a response to avoid not having one or from fear of what others might think. But now, I know that being truthful and real is always the best answer.

CHAPTER 1

OUR JOURNEY WITH FEAR AND FAITH

MY FOUNDATION IS SOLID

"My name is my purpose." - Joy

What is your foundation? What has shaped your existence and purpose? The foundation of any structure, person, and organization is key to its ability to withstand and thrive against whatever life, or the elements of the world, can bring. Your foundation is essential to what your life can endure. The elevation of your life is contingent upon this. Your goals and dreams can only be achieved with a solid foundation.

Even before I was born, my family was focused on imparting purpose in my life. They were thinking about what I would give, bring, and create. When my grandmother, Ruth, learned of my mother's pregnancy, she prayed for destiny and purpose over my life. At that time, ultrasounds were not as prevalent as they are today at revealing a baby's gender. Not knowing my gender, there was discussion as to what to name the baby. She asked God to give her a name that spoke meaning into my future. One day while sitting in church, the name *Joy* came to her spirit. Consequently, no one doubted that my mom was having a girl because the name Joy was given by God! From what I've been told, as a baby I was always a happy and smiling bundle of joy. My grandmother had a strong belief that I would bring joy not only to my family, but to anyone I encountered. In essence, she believed the world needed more joy and more happiness. This was my foundation.

Choosing a child's name bears significance. "A *good* name is rather to be chosen than great riches, and loving favour rather than silver and gold." (Proverbs 22:1 KJV) My family has a tradition in which the name of a child speaks to the existence of who and what they will bring to the world. It is not a happenstance decision but rather one that is taken with intent and forethought. In fact, my great-grandmother would often tell new mothers in the family, "You are writing the future book of your child's life based on what you name them."

Much of who I am is grounded in my faith and church experiences. I am the fourth of five generations of phenomenal women. The matriarch of my family is my maternal great-grandmother, Charity Maples. Through her union, eight talented children were born. "Gifts from God, kingdom fruit," is what she calls her children and offspring. Some of my fondest memories have been talking to her and learning about my heritage and history.

I often remember sitting on the floor listening to my great-grandmother's descriptive, less than glamorous stories of what it was like to bear children at a time when medical help was not accessible. Each time she'd share a story, she told all of the children sitting around that during each pregnancy, she prayed and asked God to bless and strengthen her body to bring forth fruit fit for his kingdom. Being the curious child that I was and having no biblical knowledge of the word "fruit," I would ask, "Grandma, what does the word fruit mean? Are you talking about fruit like we eat?" She would laugh before going into detail about how she prayed for her seeds (children) to yield a harvest of preachers, pastors, missionaries, deacons, and others to work in the church. Not only did she recite this prayer during each of her pregnancies, she prayed for future generations that had yet to come, and those prayers included *me*. I am grateful to be fruit from the vine of STRONG WOMEN. This is my foundation.

Reflection Questions:
1. Think of a memory or experience that helped define your foundation. What is it? How did it develop you into who you are today?
2. What does your name mean and how was it chosen?
3. What is your life's purpose?

DOUBT

"Faith says go as far as you can see and when you get there, you will see further. Faith is the key to remove doubt." –Taylor

D oubt is inevitable, whether evaluating the love within a relationship, worrying about your score on a test, or even questioning your faith in God. Before a wedding when people ask, "Are you getting cold feet?" they are really asking if there are any doubts.

Webster's Dictionary defines doubt as a feeling of uncertainty or lack of conviction. Doubt is like a snake lurking in the shadows of our greatest fears. It brings forth a multitude of advantages and disadvantages.

A person's doubt encourages them to seek understanding and discover truth. For example, children doubt the story of Santa Claus. The night before Christmas, thousands of kids stay up hoping to see Santa. They want him to be real.

Science is based on the premise of doubt. It teaches you how to prove a theory or a hypothesis as fact. As one begins the quest for certainty, intellect builds through knowledge and increased understanding.

William Shakespeare once said, "Modest doubt is called the beacon of the wise." Shakespeare explains that doubt in modesty is healthy and necessary to become wiser.

I doubted my parents' decision to move to Iowa. I doubted their decision even more when we got there. Simply put, the move changed me! I was no longer a happy-go-lucky ball of energy with friends and confidence. Loneliness became my new norm and it was isolating and at times overwhelming.

Quaint was an understatement when describing our two-bedroom apartment. At thirteen, I shared a tiny room with one large bed with my little brother. It's important to note that we were moving from a six-bedroom house in Memphis, TN that sat on one acre of grass-filled land. We had plenty of room to stretch our arms and now I was cramped. Just our luck, we moved to Iowa during one of the worst winters the state had seen in years. Snow, snow, and more snow. Memphis was quite the opposite as we might experience the occasional Christmas flurry that may stick around until the next morning. Therefore, Iowa was a blizzard climate that I was not prepared for. The weather was so bad that our apartment flooded not long after moving there. My doubts migrated from normal to overflowing.

Then there was my social life. My parents enrolled me in a private Lutheran middle school where there were about fifteen to twenty students in my entire grade. I'm serious! I had more friends back home than my grade had students. I was the only Black girl and I had a southern accent. This labeled me as ghetto. The students were sweet but I never felt as though I belonged. None of the girls understood me, related to me, or ever came to visit my home. All I ever wanted was to go back home to Memphis, Tennessee.

Every time someone from home would call and ask how I liked Iowa, I would lie and say, "I love it here." So, why did I lie? That's easy; I didn't want my parents to know how unhappy I felt. My mother was struggling to find her own "fit" in our new community and if she knew how I really felt, it would only make it harder for her to assimilate. They say time heals all wounds, but that was not the case for me. I switched middle schools the next year in hopes that it would alleviate some of my doubts. Again, I was wrong.

I don't think people really understand what it feels like to be the only Black girl in school when that is not what you were accustomed to, especially in a place like Iowa. Every time a school dance came around, I grew sad because I knew I was not what the boys at my school were interested in. I was a thick Black girl with curly hair and a southern twang. To compensate, I would straighten my hair, try a new diet, or even change the way I spoke. Sadly, no one asked me to a dance until my junior year of high school. In Memphis, my problems would have been non-existent. Back home, the things I tried to change would be admired. The Black boys wanted the White girls and I was "too Black" for the White boys. It wasn't just in my head either. That's actually how one of my White acquaintances explained it to me.

It pained me to have my life's circumstances shape my self-esteem, self-image, and confidence in such a negative way. Money and opportunity could not repurchase those things. Nor could they buy true friendships. I was depressed.

Now that I know what it feels like to be happy at twenty-two, I am more clear about my past reality. What was worse, no one knew. I doubted I would ever get out of that dynamic. I doubted God's plan for my life. I doubted my parents' vision for our family. I questioned my ability to be happy. Lucky for me, that wasn't my destiny nor my future. I came to understand it as a season in my life mainly meant to help me grow.

Many people begin to understand doubt through the biblical principle of faith. In the King James Bible, Hebrew 11:1 states, "Now faith is the substance of things hoped for and the evidence of things not seen." This means that faith is supposed to soothe and nourish our doubts.

Doubt is a central element when it comes to making significant decisions. Although I once faulted my parents for their decision to move to Iowa, I now appreciate their choice. Through the experience, I learned to assimilate in a culture that was once foreign. I rose above every adversity that came at me in forms of hate, jealousy, racism, and lack of understanding. I was exposed to a better educational system that prepared me with the skills to get accepted into any school of my choosing. I learned how to persevere and thrive. I learned that after you finish researching, gathering various opinions, and praying to God, it all boils down to your gut. The feeling in the pit of your stomach, once doubt has vanished and faith has kicked in. My parents relied on faith to make their decision and I cannot fault them for acting out of faith.

My story includes many more doubts along the way. However, it wasn't until I started walking by faith that I truly gained understanding. Modesty, as Shakespeare said, is truly the key to doubt because in this world, doubt is inevitable. Faith is the key to doubt and it certainly unlocked my door!

Reflection Questions:

1. Think about a time in your life where you struggled with doubt.
2. What role has faith played in your life?
3. How do you conquer doubt?

3/333333333333

EMPTY NESTING

*"Approach life changes as opportunities to grow in your marriage. It's **okay** to redefine US!"* -Ann

My husband and I are really getting on each other's nerves! I'm irritated with him, because he doesn't want to watch the television shows that I enjoy, nor do I want to watch his favorite shows (golfing, Monday night wrestling, or westerns on The Cowboy Channel). He doesn't want to go shopping, to the movies, for an afternoon walk, or read Fifty Shades of Grey, which he thinks is disgusting. (*It's an excellent book!*)

He's irritated with me because as he puts it, I "keep bugging him" to do girly stuff and watch tear-jerk movies. What is wrong with him, or maybe, what is wrong with us? We're not in sync anymore. We used to do everything together but now we seem lost or distant. Most evenings, he sits in his favorite spot on the sofa, watches television, plays on his cell phone, and falls asleep. I, on the other hand, retreat to my spot and read a book or talk on the telephone. What has happened? It's as if we are merely existing within the same walls but living separate lives or grieving some kind of loss.

Slowly, it dawns on me precisely what we are doing. We're grieving. We are feeling the emptiness and loneliness in the absence of our children, me more than him. Our nest is empty. The house is too quiet. Gone is the loud annoying music. Gone is the laughter or the chatter of voices coming from those once-occupied bedrooms of people who look like us.

It seems like only yesterday we brought each one of them home from the hospital. Where did the time go? I wasn't prepared emotionally. I thought I was okay because I didn't cry when they left. Silly of me to think tears are the only evidence of sadness. Slowly but surely, the longing grew stronger. Unaware, I've been unfairly expecting and pressuring my husband to fulfill all the voids—emptiness and loneliness, I now feel.

There are so many small things I miss. One in particular is the cooking. There is no need to cook large meals anymore. I've had to learn how to cook and prepare smaller portions which meant buying smaller pots and pans. There is no replacement like a pet or hobby that can fulfill the emptiness felt when you realize your children are gone and THE HOUSE IS EMPTY! How many times have you or your spouse said, "I can't wait for my children to become adults and move out on their own?" There comes a time in life when our long-awaited supposed happiness becomes an un-welcomed reality.

As a mother, I realize that I wrapped my life around my children. I'm appreciative that my husband understands the bond between a mother and her children. I can now see all the sacrifices of my husband who worked to finance and support the children's wants, needs, spending sprees, vacations, education, and weddings. For them, nothing is too good.

Now that our nest is empty, my husband and I need to rediscover the new "us." It's simple math; $1+1=2$, $2+2=4$, $4-2=2$. Me plus him equals "us" and "us" plus two children, equals family. The family with two grown adult children equals a return back to the original "us!"!

Reflection Questions:

1. What do you and your spouse do together, *just* with each other?

2. How have you allowed children, work, or friendships to take the front stage of your marriage/relationship? Why?

3. What immediate actions can you take to invest more quality time in your marriage/ relationship?

GOD HEARD MY PRAYER

"There is a God that answers prayers." -Joy

When I was six months pregnant, I began to experience pains that were sharp and intense. Given that my first pregnancy resulted in a miscarriage, I was extremely careful and hyper-observant of everything happening to my body. Not wanting to take any chances, I went straight to the emergency room. They hooked me up to all types of machines and told me that I was in labor. I immediately became terrified. It was too early to have my baby. The doctors officially admitted me and began medicines to stop the labor.

Over the next few weeks, I was in and out of labor. On one particular night, things got really bad and they were doing everything they could to stop the labor. I prayed and asked God to please allow me to have a healthy baby. As I prayed, a sense of calm swept over my entire body. It was a surreal moment that gave me the peace and confidence that we would both be fine.

Several days later, the hospital's head administrator called and said that he needed to meet with me and my husband to share news about my case. Although I could not put my finger on it, something about this did not sound right. When I told my husband, he refused to go as he did not want to hear *any* bad news about our baby. So, my mom decided to go to the meeting with me.

Step by step, as I walked through the office door, I spoke victory over my baby. Each step yielded a stronger level of faith. As my mother and I both sat in front of the doctor, we gave each other a nod that signaled we were going to leave victorious regardless of what the doctor shared. Let's be clear, we wanted this meeting to be over ASAP.

Here is how the conversation went:

Doctor: *Mrs. Fitzgerald, during your first trimester, you contracted a virus that most people catch as a baby. Well, unfortunately, you didn't. You caught this virus as an adult from a child in which you were exposed. Typically, this virus is a two to three-day bug that most people don't even realize they have. However, when contracted during the first trimester, the virus has a severe impact on the fetus; that is why you are going into labor. Your baby is sick. The chance of survival is less than ten percent. If you are lucky enough for the baby to live, this will be a very ill baby, and the quality of life would be seriously compromised. I would like to schedule a procedure that would allow you to terminate the pregnancy.*

Me: *Wait, let me make sure I understand what I just heard. (I looked at the doctor and then at my mother. My mother's face was one of anger. I understood her look because inside, I was just as* *upset. I looked back at the doctor.)* So, you want me to abort my baby? I just turned seven months pregnant! Are you serious?

Doctor: *I have all of the data and evidence to support this recommendation.*

(He even began to show me photos of underdeveloped babies to persuade me of the severity of my decision. With more faith and courage than I have probably ever had in my life, I looked at the doctor.)

Me: *Thank you for your concern and professional review of my medical records; however, this will not be the story of my baby. My baby will be in that ten percent and, by the way, she will not be mentally challenged, have missing organs, or be deformed. I know you don't understand my decision and I don't expect you to, but God promised me this baby and I know that he has answered my prayer.*

The doctor told me that he thought after I had time to reflect on all that he had shared, I would change my mind. To give me a safeguard, because he was confident that I would do the *right* thing, he scheduled the procedure to terminate the pregnancy for December 4th. (remember this date)

Leaving the office, my mom and I didn't utter one word. As soon as we settled in the car, she grabbed my hand, looked me in the eyes, and said, "Some things in life aren't worth repeating and this is one of them. Speaking this will only give it power. You and I both know that your baby will be fine. We are going to act like we never heard what he said. This conversation stays between us. Oh, and if I haven't told you lately, I am very proud of you!"

On the morning of December 4th, the same date in which they had scheduled to terminate my pregnancy, I woke up in severe pain. Several hours later, I was at the hospital and they were calling my doctor. He responded, "I am so glad that Joy made the right decision to terminate the pregnancy." The nurse said, "No doctor, she is in labor and dilated nine centimeters."

During my delivery, the room was full of doctors and specialists to observe my high-risk pregnancy delivery. They even provided a counselor in the delivery room to prepare for the loss and grief I might experience from the potentially severe medical complications my baby might face if she lived.

After my baby was born, the doctor said, "Oh my God Mrs. Fitzgerald! God has heard your prayer. This baby is perfect." And she was. On December 4, 1995, I became the mother of a beautiful baby girl, Taylor Simone Fitzgerald. Instead of that day being the termination of a life, it was the beginning of one. Simone has a special purpose in her name as it means, "heard by God." She is my miracle baby and the exact opposite of everything they thought she would be. She is beautiful, intelligent, gifted, talented, whole, and healthy. I am so grateful that God heard my prayer!

If you have ever experienced a tough trial in life, don't give up. One of my uncles says, "Faith says go as far as you can see, and when you get there, you will see farther." When God has promised you something, never let it go. Keep the faith regardless of what others, even doctors, might say. God hears your prayer!

Reflection Questions:
1. What are your most urgent prayers?
2. Describe a time in which you had to rely on faith.
3. What is one miracle that you have witnessed?

MY MOST EMBARRASSING MOMENT

"Never let embarrassment rule your life. It's just one moment in time." -Taylor

When I was a freshman in high school, I was the quintessential "popular nerd." Meaning, I was a chameleon amongst all the crowds. On Friday nights, I rocked the tight red and white pom-pom skirt that dug into my waist, but I also marched with the best marching band in town.

Friday nights in Iowa were devoted to high school football games, after-game celebrations at Panchero's Mexican restaurant, and the occasional teen party. I had a front row seat to it all. One minute I was shaking my pom-poms, and the next, I was jamming with the band. I lived the best of both worlds, a band geek and a pom-pom girl.

But here's where it all went wrong. This is the story of the most embarrassing thing that has happened to me.

Even though I was a freshman in high school, I was a nervous wreck when it came to the opposite sex. Instead, I left all of the bravery to my best friend, Amadi. During that stage of my life, she was my alter ego. I was the shy girl (even though my friends wouldn't have described me that way), and Amadi was the rebel afraid of nothing and no one. That was us.

One of my favorite movies was *Drumline*. From the time I saw it, I decided I wanted to be in the school band. I secretly desired that drumline and majorette romance portrayed in the movie. The problem was, I lived in White suburbia and I doubted anyone had watched the movie or even knew what a majorette was. So, I settled for pom-pom girl because it was the closest I could get to being a majorette in the Midwest.

The good news was we had a drumline in our band that I loved just like the one in the movie. I'm not sure why, but I was mesmerized by the rhythms and beats. Whenever I heard the sound of the tan sticks hit against the shiny silver brim signaling the start of a measure, I got excited. More specifically, I would get excited to see Greg Smith (that's an alias). He was a year older and, in my eyes, *SO* fine. There were only about ten Black guys in the whole school of over 2,000 students, and he was one of the cute ones.

He had pretty black curly hair, caramel colored skin, and eyes like amber. At every outdoor marching band practice, he always took his shirt off. Hello, six-pack! Sometimes I would forget the part we were playing as I stared at him. Oh, how young and boy crazy I was back then. I laugh at it now.

One morning, I decided to find Greg on Facebook since I could never seem to gain the confidence to talk to him in person. Every time he said hi, I'd giggle like an idiot. Facebook was a relatively new trend, and phone apps were not as well developed as they are now. This was the era of games like *Sorority Life* and *Farmville* (remember those?). I searched for his name but for some reason, the page would never load or bring up his profile. So, I kept doing it again, again, and again. Then I just gave up, because it was time for first period.

During class, Greg kept staring at me and even waved. I thought to myself, *Okay Tay, you must be cute today girl.* Before the period ended, I got an emergency text from Amadi telling me to meet her in the bathroom as soon as I got out of class. I knew something had happened. I thought to myself, *Shoot, did she tell him I liked him?* I wish that had been the case.

Once the bell rang, I packed up my clarinet and rushed to the bathroom. I walked in and Amadi looked like she was deciding whether or not to laugh or cry.

"What's going on?" I asked.

"Tay, I think you made a mistake and I need you to stay calm."

I could feel the lump getting bigger and bigger in my throat.

Next, she showed me my Facebook page where I had posted "Greg Smith" as my status no less than fifteen times. I thought I was going to die. Better yet, I knew I was. Instead of searching for him, I was repeatedly posting him while tagging him. OMG, this was terrible! Not only did my SECRET crush now know that I liked him, but he might now think I was a stalker. Not to mention, the whole school now knew as well.

I needed to leave. I couldn't face Greg and I certainly didn't want to see the rest of my classmates. I felt naked and afraid. Being a great best friend, Amadi took me to the nurse and I pretended to be sick. I went home suffering from the well-known illness of embarrassment.

Here's where I can admit to being a little dramatic. The next day, Greg came up to me and told me it was no big deal and that I shouldn't be embarrassed. But I was stuck in my head and I couldn't move beyond the humiliation. The very next semester, I quit the marching band. How silly is that?

Now in retrospect, I have to laugh. A couple of years ago, Greg sent me a friend request on Snapchat and from time to time, he reaches out. Sometimes I respond but most of the time, I don't. It's not that he is unattractive, it's just the older you get, you see people differently.

Thankfully, I've grown and matured. I'm not that silly little girl anymore and I learned a valuable lesson. I will never again let a boy stop me from doing something I enjoy. Greg wasn't the only reason I quit, but if I am honest, he was a large part. That was a decision I regret, and a lesson learned. Never let a man, fear of a man, or desire of a man, influence or hinder you from what you want. And certainly, don't let embarrassment get in your way!

Reflection Questions:
1. What is your most embarrassing moment and why?
2. What have you given up or stopped that you regret?
3. What caused you to give up or stop? Would you do things differently if you had the opportunity?

DON'T DO IT IF IT DOESN'T FEEL RIGHT

"If it doesn't feel right, don't do it!" -Ann

Have you ever waited for a long-desired family dream vacation, only for it to end in disaster? This was almost our fate in 2015 in Montego Bay, Jamaica. My husband, two daughters, their husbands, and three grandchildren were finally going to enjoy a beautiful tropical, week-long vacation as a family. While in flight to Jamaica, my granddaughter asked me to do something adventurous with her when we got there. I agreed as I'm now into creating memories with my grandchildren and she had a bucket list of items for the two of us.

Some months earlier in preparation for the trip, I decided to take swimming lessons because I could not swim. There was no way I was going to be on the beautiful island of Jamaica and not want to get in the water. The swimming lessons accomplished two things, and neither of which was learning how to swim. The lessons got me over the fear of the water and I learned how to float.

While relaxing and sitting on the beach one morning, we observed the many activities taking place in the ocean i.e., swimming, water skiing, and banana boat riding. My teenage grandchildren were eager and determined to get on the banana boat. After much coaxing, they got their dad and uncle to join them on the ride. I declined because I knew I could not swim. They then convinced me that it was fun and that I'd be safe because we had on life jackets, besides, all of them were excellent swimmers. I still disagreed. Then my granddaughter said, "Come on Nana, you promised." Reluctantly, I gave in.

We proceeded to the boat rental hut and began putting on our life jackets. I had an eerie feeling. My granddaughter sensing my unease said to me, "Nana don't worry. I worked one summer at the pool and became a licensed lifeguard. If you ever get in a situation where you feel as if you're drowning, all you have to do is raise your arms straight up and you'll immediately float to the top."

While at the rental hut, I asked all kinds of questions about the safety of the boat, how long was the ride, how fast would the ski boat drag the banana boat, what were the safety precautions, and what were our instructions before we left? The attendant said, there were no instructions or rules... just get on the boat and sign the waiver. Something about that did not sound right. Basically, we got on the boat at our own risk!

We boarded the banana boat, my two sons-in-law, me, my granddaughter, and my grandson. We proceeded out in the ocean at a leisure speed. My nerves were easing a tiny bit. The farther out we went, the faster the speed boat went. Now at full speed, my sons-in-law (one seated at the front and the other at the rear) began leaning and rocking the boat and splashing water. I was getting furious and begged them to stop. We were fine until the boat made a sharp turn at full speed. My sons-in-law, who were having a blast, leaned with the turn and the banana boat flipped upside down! We were all in the Pacific Ocean!

I was in the ocean, underwater, and couldn't swim! The life jacket was not pulling me up! *Ann, don't panic.* My life flashed before my eyes and I thought to myself, *"Is this how I'm going to die?"* I did not panic although I heard panicked voices all around looking for me. I could also hear my son-in-law, Tyron, telling his son (my grandson) to calm down or he would cause both of them to drown. It seemed like a lifetime, but in actuality, it was only about two minutes. Immediately, I remembered what my granddaughter told me about lifting my arms up, and when I did, I floated up and could see that I was under the boat. My other son-in-law, Alonzo, saw me and lifted me up so that my head was above the water. We all grabbed the side of the upturned banana boat and waited in the water until the ski boat returned to retrieve us.

My granddaughter and I boarded the ski boat with the drivers because I refused to get back on the banana boat. I sensed that she felt bad because she knew that I got on the banana boat ride just for her. When we made it back to the dock, I didn't care who saw or heard me. I yelled, jumped, and threw up my hands shouting, "Thank you, Jesus!"

That banana boat ride ended up being very expensive, and quite dangerous. When the boat flipped, we lost our expensive designer sunglasses and money, and I sustained a severely sprained finger. I learned a valuable lesson, I will never put my life or safety at the mercy of others or be a participant of, or in, anything about which I am uneasy. If it doesn't feel right, nine times out of ten, it isn't right! I advise anyone when traveling to other countries, be careful and cautious because safety regulations are not required or practiced as strictly as they are in the U.S.

Our family's dream vacation ended on a good note and we enjoyed ourselves and look forward to doing it again! However, I won't ever be caught on another banana boat.

Reflection Questions:
1. Think about a time when you did something that didn't feel right. Why did you do it?
2. How do you deal with uncertainty? Do you panic, remain calm, etc.?
3. What lessons have "intuition" taught you?

WIDOW AT 32

"My joy is my strength." -Charity

I met my children's father and husband at a picnic. Back in the day, we had groups like what you currently refer to as sororities. Our sororities were called Number Nine and Number Thirteen. They had uniforms and everything. Often, they would host picnics and invite people to attend. To make it easy for everyone to find, the picnics were always held on the church grounds.

One day after attending Number Thirteen's picnic, I walked home. The plantation on which I lived, had a fence around it with a gate that we called a gap. I looked up and saw a rather good-looking young man in front of me with a few other boys walking through the gap. He headed north and I headed east. He began chunking rocks at me, which got my attention. I turned around and thought, *He looks alright to me.* I slowed down as I noticed him walking back to the gap. As he approached, he began talking to me. His name was Perry Joe Austin Maples.

Perry was handsome and as some might say "nice on the eyes." As he spoke, I was somewhat mesmerized and captivated by his approach. He was confident. He asked when he could see me again. My answer was the second and fourth Sunday of the month.

He showed up the following Sunday at the church that I attended. He asked if he could walk me home, while blushing and smiling, I was happy to say yes. Our parents let us have company at the house up until 9 p.m.; however, there was one rule. The boys had to have their shirts buttoned up and tucked inside their pants. We were allowed to have two boyfriends. It's not like children are today as they only date one person. One boy would see me on the first and third Sunday, and the other boy would spend time with me on the second and fourth Sunday. They would walk me home after church and hold my hand. That's how we had company. I wasn't in love with either of the guys; that was not the goal.

The girls in my neighborhood were jealous of Perry and I dating. One even told me, "If you want your man, you better pin him to your side because if he flags my train, I am going to let him ride." You know what I told her? "I ain't worried bout that." I knew Perry wanted me and I wanted him. Not long after falling in love, we got married.

Because Perry's dad died when he was young, we didn't have much help. Perry had to work on the Bob White farm to take care of us. He was hired to do odds and ends type of jobs. He wasn't a sharecropper because we didn't live on the farm. Instead, Perry would go by every day to see if work was needed and then he would be paid for a day's work.

Perry was an outgoing man and often did things that weren't good for him. He couldn't drink alcohol, because it would make him sick. However, my husband liked women. One day, he went somewhere (I guess to another woman's house) and ate some bad food and it caused appendicitis.

The doctor told him that his appendix needed to be removed. Being concerned with work and pay, Perry asked if he could finish his crop before having the surgery. By the time he finished, he was in so much pain that he laid down beside the crop, barely able to move. Trying to feel better, he took some black draw and castor oil, which only made it worse. Unfortunately, his appendix burst. We tried to get him to go to the hospital and by the time he finally went, it had poisoned his whole body. They gave him only days to live.

I was thirty-two years of age and pregnant when I became a widow. With seven children, pregnant and no husband, I felt terrible and afraid. I didn't have anyone to talk to and I couldn't talk to my sister as she made me feel worse. Unfortunately, I kept my most vulnerable feelings and fears to myself. The night my husband passed, the Lord told me, "I am with you." God has been with me all the way, and he has kept me and my eight children.

I never remarried. I didn't want to repeat the experience I had as a child by bringing another parent into the home of my children who might not love or show them respect. I had four boys and couldn't fathom the thought of bringing another man into the house for them to call dad. No, I wouldn't do it.

I was young, nice looking, and had options as it related to men. But, I chose to remain a widow at thirty-two because I believed the sacrifice was best for my family tree. I wanted the tree to remain rooted in the Maples name and family. I didn't want to uproot what had been placed in my home.

It wasn't easy. I was afraid many days and nights. Although I didn't know how we would survive, I always knew God was with me. I now look back over my life and know that the joy of the Lord was and is MY STRENGTH.

Imagine raising eight children without any help. Can you fathom being totally dependent on your husband and waking up one day and there are seven sets of eyes looking to you to take care of them and provide answers? Well, with a great deal of faith and strength, I did it. I kept my family together. I worked and raised my eight children to be productive men and women in the world.

I want women to know that whatever you are going through, you can make it. Don't give up. There were times when I questioned if I was strong enough to do this by myself. I had no choice. I had eight children who needed a strong mother. Women if you ever feel down or low, know that God is a sustainer and strong tower. Pray and trust in Him, and He will bring you through.

If you ever become single and you have children, be very careful who you bring into their company. This can make or break them. As a woman, you might have to sacrifice your needs and wants to ensure the safety, security, and success of your family. Not one day have I regretted my decision. I genuinely believe I made the right choice. Be encouraged and know that strength lies in you.

Reflection Questions:
1. What has been your greatest struggle in life?
2. What has brought you the greatest joy? And why?
3. How have you dealt with death or a significant loss?

CHAPTER 2

OUR JOURNEY IN CULTURE

MY NAME IS NOT MARY

"It doesn't matter what people call you; it matters what you answer to."-Ruth

Names are very important. In fact, half of our daily conversations consist of names — people, places, and things. What would you be called if you didn't have a name? Or what would people call you if they didn't know your name?

I often hear people mispronounce a person's name, now more than ever because we live in a diverse and multicultural society. I think when you meet someone for the first time and you're unsure of how to phonetically pronounce or enunciate their name, you should ask them to say it slowly, attentively listen, and then attempt to repeat what they've said. It is disrespectful to mispronounce a person's name knowingly. Some people have the audacity to unapologetically assign you a nickname rather than to learn your name. The nickname is easier for them and often hides their inability to pronounce a name. The ultimate form of disrespect is not even desiring to know a person's name, and instead choosing to brand or label them by biased terms such as that *Jew lady*, *African lady*, or *those people*.

As I reflect, it's 1945, and I'm at home with my mother and siblings in our small three-room farmhouse. It is a normal, uneventful summer day. My father is a farmer and loves to hunt deer, rabbits, quail, and raccoons. He often goes out at night hunting with his numerous hunting dogs. In fact, at one time, he owned fifteen dogs and he knew each one of them by name.

He really loves and cares for his dogs. It is my job to cook biscuits and feed them, which I hate with a passion. (I'm certain this is the reason that I don't like dogs to this day, because we had so many and I had to feed them.)

A knock on the door interrupts and shifts our normal, uneventful day. My mother answers to find a man standing on the other side of the threshold. I notice that she does not invite him in, nor does he attempt to enter the house. They talk. I decipher that he is looking for my father and somebody else by the name of Mary. My mother tells him that my father is not at home. But I'm wondering who is this Mary that he keeps talking about?

He continues to talk, uses the name Mary, and inquire about wanting to buy one of my father's dogs. I listen intently, because I want to know about Mary. Surely, he's not calling my mother Mary. I finally realize that he is in fact calling my mother Mary. Why isn't she correcting him? She knows that her name is not MARY! And more importantly, why is she answering to this name? Their conversation finally ends. He says, "Well thank you Mary. Tell your husband I came by." She says okay, nods, and shuts the door.

"Momma, why was that man calling you Mary?"

That day, she explained to me the difference between "White folks" and "colored folks." She said, "Ruth, Mary is the name White folks call all colored women." Confused I asked, "Why?" She said, "It's just the way things are."

This average, uneventful day suddenly became a poignant, pivotal day in my life that I will never forget. I was angry and upset. I knew that as Black folk, we were treated differently and less than, but we deserved a name! I could not believe that my mom would answer to a name that didn't belong to her. What was so wrong and so bad with being Black that we didn't even deserve the dignity of having a unique identity such as a name? It was then that I decided I would never answer to a name that was not mine. I wanted the world to know that MY NAME IS NOT MARY, MY NAME IS RUTH; I at least deserve that!

Reflection Questions:
1. Have you ever felt marginalized in life? When and why?
2. How did you handle the situation? Did you stand up for yourself or did you relent and give up keeping the peace? If so, why or why not?
3. Describe your "true" self if no one was watching? Why do you hide pieces and parts of yourself?

ONE DAY IT WILL BE MY TABLE

"One day I will get to rewrite history at my table."
-Taylor

This is one no one knows, not even my parents. It was 2012, my sophomore year of high school, and we lived in Cedar Rapids, Iowa. I felt Black, was frightened to be Black, and knew that my Black father could potentially go to jail if he ever knew this story.

My best friends and I were invited to a friend's house to spend the night. The friend, let's refer to her as Hannah, was White. My Black best friend and I were having fun listening to music and playing in makeup when a knock came at Hannah's door.

As she opened the door to find her dad standing there, my instincts were suddenly on high alert. It was the piercing look he had in his eyes. He looked at my best friend and I as if we were trash spreading an odor throughout his house. He told Hannah to come into the hall where we overheard him explain, "Dinner is ready, but Black people (he used the N-word) are not welcomed at my kitchen table."

He told Hannah we could eat in her room if we were hungry but I was no longer hungry. Surprisingly, I wasn't even scared of him; I was embarrassed. I was ashamed that I was in the situation, shocked that I actually heard what I heard, and nervous to tell my mom why I needed to be picked up immediately. There was only one thing I could do. I lied. I told my mom I was cramping and that I needed to be picked up ASAP.

I never went to Hannah's house again. I never forgot that my Black skin still mattered and I never told my parents. I'm sharing this story because on that day, I realized to be Black in America and have opportunities is still a struggle. Sadly, inclusion is a gift, not a right.

It was 2012 and I was STILL not welcome at the table. That day I made it my mission to be the best version of myself because one day I will have my own table, and my choices will be different.

Reflection Questions:
1. Have you ever personally experienced racism? How did you feel?
2. How did you deal with your feelings?
3. What lessons did you learn about you? And others?

GUESS WHO'S COMING TO DINNER

"I never thought I would be invited to a White man's table." - Ruth

I have lived in Memphis my entire adult life. The south is home and a place in which I find comfort. In 2007, my granddaughter, Joy and her family relocated to Cedar Rapids, Iowa. While I could not believe they were living in Iowa of all places, I was happy with the job opportunities that it was providing for her family.

To help them get settled, I offered to go and stay with them for a month. While Iowa was different, I grew to like the simplicity and safety of the small city. One day, Tyron, Joy's husband, said that his boss had invited us to his home for dinner. I immediately thought, *Well, that doesn't include me.* I guess he could read my thoughts because he said, "And that includes you too grandma." I didn't want to go, but I didn't want to hurt their feelings.

The next day, we packed up in the minivan and headed to the home of his boss. We pulled up and I could feel my chest getting tight as I was so nervous. I didn't know how to tell Tyron and Joy that I didn't feel comfortable doing this. I held in my feelings and put a smile on my face. Once we got inside, I noticed that we were the only Black family there.

They all began to talk and socialize. I sat on the couch and didn't say one word. Truth be told, I was afraid that I wasn't articulate enough to join the conversation. I was scared that my southern accent would be too heavy and they would judge me. So, I decided it was best not to speak. When we all went to the dining room table, I noticed the lovely décor and the food looked terrific. I got even more nervous. *Why did Joy and Tyron do this to me? Did they know how I was feeling?* Apparently not, as they were laughing and talking and not paying me any attention.

I barely ate my food as I had lost my appetite. I felt out of place, as if I didn't belong. I decided to leave the table and go into the next room to be by myself. *Whew,* I thought to myself, *this felt so much better.* I had only been in the room for five minutes when Steve, Tyron's boss, came in and sat on the couch with me. Now I was even more uncomfortable which I think he sensed. He then did everything he could to make me feel comfortable. He began to ask about the children. Now that was easy and a topic that I enjoyed.

When we left, Tyron said, "That was really nice. I had a great time."

"Me too," everyone agreed.

"Grandma, why are you so quiet? You were different at the house. Were you okay?" asked Taylor.

"No, I was not okay. That was not a pleasant dinner for me."

"Grandma, why did you not have a good time? Everyone was so nice. Steve even went out of his way to make you feel comfortable. I don't' get it," commented Joy.

"You're right. I guess you don't get it. Do you know that was the first time in my entire life that I was invited to sit at the table of a White man and eat? I have cooked for White people my whole life and no one has ever invited me to their table to eat. It was so uncomfortable and strange. I never thought in my entire life that I would have this experience. I was worried about what I would say and more importantly, if I would embarrass you guys."

"Grandma you could never embarrass us. I'm shocked. I would have never thought this experience was that different for you. I guess Steve recognized it and that's why he came and talked to you," said Joy.

"That was really nice of him. See, you kids have been conditioned to be comfortable around White people. You have been exposed and in settings where you have gained skills and confidence in talking to them. You have had the pleasure and privilege to be in integrated school systems. You guys grew up being treated differently. That is not my journey. I grew up at a time where White folks treated Blacks worse than dogs. We didn't have rights; we didn't have access to a good educational system. They weren't our friends; we were their servants. You see baby, how can you ever befriend and trust a person that never did anything worth trusting? That is the conditioning and experiences I had during childhood. So, the possibility of what you guys are enjoying, never was a reality for me. Now, I get to share new experiences with you that are different and it will take me a while to get comfortable with the uncomfortable."

Throughout life, each of us have different experiences that shape who we are and how we see the world. Those experiences can prepare and equip us to be successful in various environments. Quite the opposite, a lack of experiences can leave us ill-prepared and exposed in navigating successfully in different situations.

It is important to expose yourself to as many environments in life as possible. This will help to expand your worldview. It is critical that you prepare your children through exposure to different experiences, cultures, belief systems, and ethnicities so they have the proper conditioning to experience and value the diversity of the world.

Reflection Questions:
1. Describe a time in your life where you felt "different."
2. What did you learn from Ruth's experience?
3. Are there people in your family who see the world differently than you? How can you help to expand their worldview?

I PRAY WE BECOME A BETTER WORLD

To truly be inclusive, the world needs more love and understanding. – Joy

At a time when the racial climate in the United States is continually being depicted on the news, radio, and TV, I have tried my best to remain hopeful, encouraged, and unbothered. It has been hard! But, I persevere.

On a beautiful day last week, I was driving home from work. The sun was shining, it was seventy degrees, and I was feeling great. It was so pretty outside that I had the windows down and I was enjoying the picturesque, quiet ride home, using the opportunity to reflect on the day's events. I was feeling grateful.

I live in Carmel, a small suburb in Indianapolis that has a European feel. You literally can't drive two miles without having to engage in a roundabout.

As I was driving in the downtown area of Carmel, the traffic was somewhat at a standstill due to the roundabout. While sitting still, I noticed two Caucasian children, a boy and a girl, standing at the corner waving at each driver as he or she approached. They looked to be between the ages of nine to twelve.

Sitting in my car observing two adorable, carefree children, standing outside offering a kind gesture to individuals made me smile. Without fail, a car approached and the children smiled and waved. Then the next car approached, and they smiled and waved. The pattern continued.

That is, until I approached. When I got up to where they were, I received a rude and offensive response. The little boy, who appeared to have been nine or ten years old, looked directly at me and raised both hands in the air, flipped me the bird, and then stuck out his tongue. The older sister then followed her brother's actions and repeated the same gestures. I was stunned and honestly speechless!

I looked around to confirm that I was really witnessing what I already knew my eyes had seen. I even tried to see if they were objectifying this sentiment at anyone else other than me. The answer was NO. I will never forget the vile look of disrespect the younger boy had as he looked me straight in my face.

I pulled over to the side of the road and parked. I had to understand if this was the way others were greeted too. I sat as six other cars approached and they were each greeted with a smile and a wave. So, what was different? They were White and I was Black. I was bothered to my core!

But why? Why was I allowing it to affect me? Why did it hurt? They are just children, and I knew I was bigger than that gesture or their contempt. Suddenly, I became sad. Really sad. As I reflected, I understood why it bothered and hurt me. It was different. It was different because they were innocent kids. We tell ourselves racism rests in the older generation and that our children are our future. *This* reality of the future horrified me.

I felt bad for those children. Their behavior was learned. They were not born that way. I work in diversity and inclusion. Theirs were actions that I should be able to ignore and chalk off as nothing, but I couldn't. It was different, because it reflected our future! I felt sorry for those children because someone had failed them. Someone had not taught them to show respect and dignity for all people. It saddened me that one day, they will be in business or corporate America. They will have learned how to mask these overt actions to subtle everyday micro-inequities that seek to exclude, disrespect, and devalue people who look like me. Those actions will be articulated as "unconscious" when in fact they are very "conscious" and aware of their intentions.

It was a signal that we have a long way to go. Our greatest opportunity is to impact and infuse more love and inclusive behaviors in our children. They will be the catalyst for a new society and a better world where all people can experience respect and inclusion. Let's pray they are.

Reflection Questions:
1. Have you ever experienced racism or bias? If so, how did it impact you?
2. Do you pray for the world? If so, what is your prayer?
3. What surprised you most when reading this story?

CHAPTER 3

FINDING JOY AFTER LOSS

SURVIVING THE DEATH OF MY CHILD

"Remember the good times and keep thanks in your heart; that's your peace." - Ruth

Loss is defined as the fact or process of losing something or someone. Although it is a four-letter word, it carries the weight of complex meaning. Loss is difficult to comprehend or understand.

Many have said to me over the last couple of years, "Mrs. Givens, I am so sorry for your loss." I hear those words and I think to myself, my son's death is not a loss. "For to me, to live is Christ, and to die is gain." (Philippians 1:21 KJV)

There was no preparation or warning for my son's death. I was not ready. We were not ready. Kelvin was my first son. As a child, he was always happy with a big heart and bright smile. Kelvin was a kind person and cared about everyone. If he ever carried a fault, it was that he was too nice at times. He was the kind of person that wherever he went, he made friends. I guess you could say he was a people person. He loved serving the church and helping others. There was nothing I ever asked him to do that he didn't do. He was a good son and made me and his father proud.

Being the helper that he was, after his father died, he always made sure that my needs were met. He stepped in where his father left off by protecting me and doing the "manly" things around the house such as cutting the grass, fixing things, and making sure that I had whatever I needed. I never had to ask; Kelvin just did what he felt needed to be done. He looked out not just for me, but for everybody. That was my boy.

One day, Kelvin came by the house to cut the yard and install a new stove. We did our typical mother/son things and caught up on his life and his children. I remember at one point during our conversation, he looked at me, smiled and said, "Mom, I am really happy!" His words brought joy to my heart because Kelvin had gone through some things in the church that I knew hurt him. It was good to see him at peace.

We even laughed about his weight as he and Diane (his wife) had been on a health kick and he had lost a lot of weight. He was looking good. He was so proud of his weight loss that he bought himself a couple of new suits and brought them over for me to alter.

While he worked, I talked and altered his clothes. It was our special time, just me and him. Once he was done, he told me that he and Diane were heading out of town for a little vacation. After my husband died, we had this little rule that if one of us ever went out of town, we had to tell the other one where we were going so that we wouldn't worry. So, Kelvin was telling me about his plans.

He said goodbye and headed to the car. I walked down the hallway and saw his suits hanging on the door. I ran to the door to stop him but noticed that he was almost at his car. I decided I wouldn't bother him because I knew he needed to get home as he was heading out of town.

Walking to his car is the last visual memory I have of Kelvin. He was happy, really happy! In retrospect, I guess God knew that I needed that to be my last memory, hearing my son talk about how happy he was. That is how I will always remember him, happy and at peace.

Later that night, I woke up to my phone ringing at about 2 a.m. It was Diane telling me that they couldn't wake Kelvin up. Confused I said, "What do you mean you can't wake him up?" She kept repeating the same thing, "We can't wake Kelvin up." Disoriented, half asleep, and in shock, I told her to hang up the phone so I could get myself together and that I would call her back. I then called my other three children and shared what little information I had.

Once I got myself somewhat together, I called Diane back. She told me that he woke up in the middle of the night gasping for breath and stopped breathing. I became numb.

Words do little to explain my feeling at that moment. It was indescribable and unfamiliar. I had lost a husband, but that was nothing compared to losing my child. I thought losing my husband of fifty-four years was hard, but there is a different level of grief and pain that you feel in the pit of your stomach and all over your body when it is your child. That was my baby, my child. Not Kelvin! NOT Kelvin! Lord please, NOT KELVIN!

He was a part of me. How was I going to deal with the loss? I needed to be strong but I was numb. I trusted and served God faithfully but Kelvin's death did not make sense. I didn't know how to feel or express my feelings. I had gotten to a place where I just wanted to scream and not stop screaming. But a little calming voice would always say, "Don't go there. If you do, you might not come back. You know you have got to come back. It is going to be too hard if you let yourself go there." God was talking to me because I had never had those thoughts in my mind before.

I stayed calm and quiet for months as I was hurting on the inside. As a mother, I tucked my feelings away and worried about my other three children, Ann, Lorraine, and Lee. I worried about Diane and his five children. How were they going to cope without their father? I guess you could say that I poured myself into fixing everyone else so that I didn't have to deal with fixing me.

One day as I sat on the side of my bed, I spoke these words: "Lord, what can I do to make myself feel better? Kelvin is gone and I know that you took him. I have got to live without him, so please tell me what I can do to make myself feel better?" God spoke to me and said, "Just say thank you." I thought to myself, *Now Lord, I am not ready for that. I am not there yet.* My mind didn't want to do it. How can I be thankful when my son is dead? I was not ready on that day or several days later.

As time continued to pass, I would think about all the wonderful memories I had with my child. Kelvin was a grown man to everyone else, but to me, he was still my baby. Little by little and day by day, I thanked the Lord for allowing me to have the wonderful gift of being Kelvin's mother. I thanked Him for the life that Kelvin had, the service and leadership he gave to the church, the heart he shared with everyone, the acts of kindness that he gave that blessed so many people, the light that he was to our family, the souls that he brought to Christ, and the wife and children who remain here. I became grateful that God didn't allow him to be sick or suffer. Instead, He took him peacefully in his sleep.

I had so much to be grateful and thankful for. Before I knew it, I was saying "thank you" repeatedly. The more I said it, the better I felt. This was my deliverance. This was the answer to my prayer.

I still miss my son. There is not a day that goes by that I don't think about Kelvin. He was a special child and gift to me and the world. I know he loved me and he knew that I loved him. So, when people ask, "How do you survive your child's death?" I first explain that grief is a hard and long journey that takes time. However, I am a living testimony that you can conquer grief and be happy. Kelvin would not want me to be sad and living a life of misery. That is not who he was and that is not who I am.

I still have my moments, but when I do, I reflect and remember all the wonderful things about him and his life and before I know it, there is a "thank you" that comes up in my spirit. As I share my story, I pray for all the many men and women who are struggling with grief, especially parents. I pray that God gives you peace.

I know that when people die, they refer to them as a loss. But my son is not a loss; he is a gain into the kingdom of heaven. He fought a good Christian fight, and now he is resting as his work here on earth is WELL DONE and I remain THANKFUL.

Reflection Questions:
1. What is the deepest hurt you have experienced?
2. Why was this the deepest?
3. How have you coped or dealt with hurt or grief? (Avoidance, denial, confronting, counseling, etc.)

MISCARRIAGES AND ANGELS IN THE SKY

"God's will is perfect, even when it is difficult for me to accept." – Joy

For as long as I can remember, I always wanted to be a mother. As a little child, I loved dolls and I looked forward to Sundays where I would attend church and hold all of the beautiful babies.

As you can imagine, not long after being married, I wanted a baby. So, my husband and I set out on the journey to conceive. I was so excited that I would brush my tongue extra-long amounts of time just waiting to feel some sense of nausea to indicate that I might be pregnant. How crazy is that?

Well one day, I was experiencing bladder issues and went to the doctor and learned that I was two months pregnant. I was ecstatic! I found a cute romantic way to share the wonderful news with my husband. He too was overjoyed and jumped on the phone and one by one, called all of his friends and family members to share our great news. He was going to be a dad. We were thrilled.

A month and a half later, I was in the den vacuuming when I felt a sharp pain at the lower part of my stomach. It was so severe and different that I immediately laid down on the couch and called my mom. She assured me that everything was fine and to just rest and not worry.

Throughout the night, I continued to hurt. I called my doctor and he said, "Pain is normal, don't worry." The next morning when I got ready for work, I went to the restroom and saw blood. Fear erupted in my soul. I was scared that I was losing my baby. I tried my best to have positive thoughts, but I was terrified. My heart was beating hard as fear engulfed me. As I stood looking at the blood, I gained the strength to yell for my husband's help. He entered the bathroom, kissed me, and told me that we needed to go straight to the hospital.

The journey to the hospital was long and hard, and I wanted to make this go away so badly. When we arrived, the on-call doctor examined me and said that everything was okay. Something in my gut said otherwise. I asked if I could stay for a couple of hours to be observed. The doctor assured me that everything was fine, but to calm my nerves, he agreed to let me stay under observation for a while.

Several hours later, he came back, examined me again, and could not find a heartbeat anymore. He then did an ultrasound, and we learned that I was experiencing a miscarriage. I remember the look on my husband's face. It was a look that I will never forget. Our hearts were broken. It was the first time I saw my husband broken. This added to the devastation, as I had always seen him as my pillar of strength.

I was crushed and felt as if it was my fault. We both stayed in bed for days and held each other. Weeks later, I began to question my ability to ever have children. Self-doubt crept into my soul making me feel less than a woman. It was even harder to deal with my miscarriage as my sister was pregnant and expecting her baby. I needed to be happy for her, but it was hard as I was dealing with my own grief.

Every time I saw a baby, I cried. Every time I saw a pregnant woman, I questioned, "Why not me?" Why had God taken my baby? What about all the girls and women who were unfit and didn't desire a child, why did they get to have their babies?

IT WAS NOT FAIR!

I looked at my husband and often wondered if he would still want me if I could never have children. Would he still love me the same? Would he be open to adoption? Those were the questions that I pondered over and over.

I became obsessed with having a baby. My husband encouraged me to seek counsel from someone who had gone through the experience. I talked to a lady who had experienced five miscarriages. She encouraged me to separate having a child with being a mother or being a woman. Those things were not synonymous. More importantly, she told me that I was complete and whole whether I was able to have children or not.

This story is special as it marks a dark and sad time in my life. I am grateful for two living children and for the two angels (miscarriages) that God gave me. Miscarriages are more common than we think. It is power in us sharing our stories of loss, grief, and sorrow with other women. It helps us to know that we are not alone and that there is triumph behind travail.

To all the women who have struggled with infertility, miscarriages, stillbirths, or infant deaths, be encouraged that it was not your fault. You are not stained or being punished.

In God, you are never barren. You were created to give birth, and that can take place in many forms. You have the ability to birth love, joy, peace, goodness, and hope into the lives of so many of God's children.

If you have experienced a miscarriage, God has given you a special angel in the sky! I confirm and speak inspiration to your spirit to know that you are beautifully and wonderfully made just as you are.

Reflection Questions:
1. What parts of this story did you connect with and why?
2. If you experienced infertility or loss of a child, how did you cope with your emotions?
3. What experiences have you had that could help another woman heal? What is your story?

A MOTHER'S LOVE

"Everyone needs to experience the love of a mother." - Charity

My mother passed when I was one year and eleven months old. I don't have a visual memory of how she looked. But, I remember being held and loved by her. I vividly recall when she died. She was lying in bed and I tried to lie down with her. One of my sisters pulled me away and wouldn't let me touch her. I was too young to understand this moment in time. I had no clue that this surreal moment would impact me for the rest of my life in ways I couldn't imagine.

In 1919, they did not embalm bodies like they do today. So, the very next day, my mom was buried. My father returned home and prepared a meal for my siblings and me. We all sat/stood around the table while my father prayed over the food. He then looked into the warmer (this is what we called the stove) and pulled out some bread. He said, "Your mom cooked this bread and I think we should eat it." I think it was his way of saying goodbye. I looked around at my brothers and sisters and all I saw was sadness. Being a toddler, I had no clue of the gravity of what was happening and how this would be a critical loss in all our lives.

Over the next couple of days, two of our aunts came to live with us for a while. I assume they were fulfilling their family obligation to help my dad with all the children. My aunts were different. They were not my mom. While I may not be able to remember much about her, I knew I was loved. I knew the touch of her hand. I knew what it felt like to be hugged and gently cared for. Now, everything felt different.

The very next month, I turned two years old. While I can't quite remember how it happened, I got a button stuck in my nose. I went for help but got a reaction I didn't expect. My aunt looked at me with fury as she raised her hand in the air and slapped me in my face. Imagine a 160-pound adult woman slapping a two-year-old in the face. I was scared and hurt. I needed my mom but I didn't know where she was and it felt like she was never coming back.

Within a couple of months, my father came home and told us that he was getting a mother for us. We got excited because we wanted a mother, someone to love and care for us. One day, we were all standing in the yard waiting for our father to return home with our new mom. We were dressed in our best clothes and wanted to make a good impression. I remember her walking up to the yard. She had on brown shoes and carried a hen under her arm. She walked up to each of us and spoke. We called her *mama down home*. We were all grinning from ear-to-ear as this was a new beginning, and we were hopeful that she was going to be a good mother.

We were wrong.

For ninety-five years, I held my truth in my heart and I shared it with no one. The truth is, I grieved my entire life for a mother's love. I mourned the loss of my mother. My stepmother never gave me a mother's love and only did enough to make sure I had the basic needs in life. Sometimes, that was an issue. I often felt mistreated and unloved by her. I remember being about four years old. All my other siblings would leave home each day and head to school. Once they left, my stepmom would get a small stool and sit me in the corner. I would have to stay in that corner all day until my siblings arrived home. They would rescue me and take care of me.

Can you imagine being a little girl and NEVER having a memory of your mother combing or brushing your hair? She may have only done it once. She never even washed my clothes or gave me a bath. I couldn't understand it. Thankfully, my dad loved me and tried his best to compensate for the lack of love I received. He would comb my hair and try to take care of me. There was not a day that went by that I didn't long for love. I wanted to feel accepted and cared for; instead, I felt isolated. I never got hugs or affection like most children. My sisters did the best they could. They would comb my hair. It would be so tight that I would have big red bumps all over my scalp. Again, I felt abandoned and alone.

You might ask, why did it take me ninety-five years to share my truth? Honestly, I sacrificed my feelings for my dad and my children. If my children were aware of how I was treated, it would impact how they viewed both my dad and stepmom. I didn't want that for them. I safeguarded the truth so they could have a relationship with the both of them. I didn't want to start their young lives with hate and resentment because of my experiences. I am 100 years old and the last one living of my siblings. I decided to share this now because it can't hurt any of them. Because I want people to know the power of love or loss of love.

No one can replace a mother's love. My older sisters tried. Papa tried, but it wasn't the same. There was always a longing and deep need that went unfulfilled. I missed that in my childhood. I didn't have a mom to call or ask for advice when I became an adult because I didn't have that type of relationship with anyone. I was on my own. I made a vow early in life that I would be different. I would give my children what I never had, a mother's love. You can learn from everyone and I learned who I didn't want to be. That is the gift that my stepmom gave me.

Reflection Questions:
1. Describe your relationship with your mother.
2. How has your relationship with your mother impacted your life?
3. What lessons have you learned from your mother or lack thereof?

MY MEMORY BOX

"Memories are reminders that give us evidence of our journey." -Ann

I'm a collector of precious keepsakes and none are more valuable to me than those that belong, or once belonged, to a loved one. I even have a house plant that I've kept alive for almost forty years. I call "her" Mother Robinson. Mother Robinson is a philodendron that I collected at a funeral of a dear old church mother whose name happened to be Mother Robinson. Now, alongside Mother Robinson on my kitchen floor, in beautiful flower pots, sit "Big Daddy" (my father-in-law) and Kelvin (my brother). These common house plants mean nothing to the casual observer, but to me, they are perpetual memories of loved ones that I care for each week.

It's 2007, my daughter and her family are breaking a family norm by moving away to Iowa. No one in our close-knit family has ever ventured to uproot and relocate to another state. Mind you, my entire family lives within a twenty-mile radius of each other. Although there were many opportunities and lucrative offers during my husband's career to move and relocate, we both decided there were too many family connections and obligations to move away. So, we stayed.

I was devastated at the news of them moving and being so far away. I would miss my daughter, son-in-law and young grandchildren. I would miss seeing them grow up and being a part of their lives. My way of coping with this inevitable sadness was to ignore and compartmentalize their move and not talk about it. I secretly thought they would never go, or that a change of mind would soon come. Reality finally arrived one day in the form of a moving truck.

Realizing our sadness (mine and theirs), my daughter, son-in-law, and grandchildren came up with an excellent idea. On their first return visit after the move, they gifted me with a beautiful gold jewelry box. Inside the jewelry box were several hand-written personal notes, different sizes, different colors, and in their different handwritings. They had made me a "memory box." In their notes, each of them detailed times, memories, encouraging words, and expressions of love. They said, "Each time you feel sad and miss us, open the memory box and read one of the notes. It will bring a smile to your face and know that we are near." Overwhelmed with emotion, I was speechless and could only cry considering how much thought, time, and effort had gone into making something so beautiful and precious. Truthfully, the memory box helped me adjust to not having them physically near me but kept them ever present in my heart and as near as a simple little note.

Since that time, each Christmas they add a new handwritten memory, card, or letter to the box. The memory box is a dose of happiness I give myself when I am down or want to feel special or close to my family. It is one of the most valuable items that I possess and just like "Mother Robinson," "Big Daddy," and "Kelvin," the memory box has its permanent place as a "keepsake" in my heart.

Reflection Questions:
1. What are the memories or items that you hold dear from the past? Why?
2. What memories make you happy? Which make you sad?
3. Write a story to someone that could serve as a memory of inspiration.

OBEDIENCE IS BETTER THAN SACRIFICE

"It is better to obey than to experience great sacrifice." - Charity

I had two twin older siblings, Naomi AD, and Ruth LC. Now you might ask, what do the letters AD and LC stand for? Well, nothing. I guess back in the olden days, initials or single letters of the alphabet were used as names.

After maternal death took the life of my mom and younger brother, my dad (Papa) remarried and my siblings and I were forced to accept that she could never replace our mother.

Life without our mom was hard on all of us but it was particularly difficult for one of the twins, Ruth. Ruth struggled with my stepmom. She didn't like her and chose to rebel as a demonstration of her feelings. Papa was a man of faith and often talked to Ruth about her behavior and lack of respect for *mama down home*. He would quote the biblical scripture, "Children, obey your parents in the Lord: for this is right. Honour thy father and mother; which is the first commandment with promise; That it may be well with thee, and thou mayest live long on the earth." (Ephesians 6:1-3 KJV)

Ruth continued to be disobedient. I guess you could say she had her own way of doing things. Papa would often discipline and remind her, "Disobedient children don't live past their days." That was his articulation of the biblical scripture. During this time, I was young, but I remember the constant struggle to get Ruth to be more accepting and obedient.

One day, we were given a chore to get water from the well. We took the buggy along with several pails to get water to bring back to the house. Papa instructed each of us to be careful and told us what to avoid while carrying the buckets. He warned us of the potential damage we could face if we didn't follow his instructions.

As usual, Ruth did things her way. She got two pails and filled each pail to the top with water. She then jumped down with one pail in each hand, both legs flat without bending her knees. She fell to the ground. I knew she was hurt. She got up and tried to pretend she was okay. We later went to a picnic, but Ruth was not doing well. She got sick. So, we decided to return home.

Ruth's stomach became extremely swollen, and she was in a great deal of pain. She had torn something in her body. Papa laid Ruth on the bed and began to pray. We were all scared. The doctor soon came and said she had torn her intestines. Ruth suffered for a couple of days in pain. Seeing Ruth suffer was hard on my dad.

Ruth began to hurt even more and needed relief as her stomach got bigger and bigger. The doctor had instructed us that there was nothing he could do. My dad got a knife. He scorched and sanitized the knife. He then pierced Ruth's stomach to try to give her some relief. He put a pail near the incision and tons and tons of fluid drained into the bucket. While this gave her some relief, she was still suffering.

We all stood around her bed watching her minute by minute. She started to sing and pray. She said everything looked dark to her but after she prayed, the light returned, and the darkness had gone away. She then looked at her twin sister Naomi and said, "Today is my last day on this earth and I am glad." She looked around at each one of us and said, "Make sure you are obedient and do what *mama down home* and Papa tells you to do because I was disobedient." Within minutes, she closed her eyes and she was gone. Before she died, she tried to get dad to pray, but he couldn't. I think it was too much for him to face.

I lived with her testimony. Ruth was only fourteen. It shaped how I lived because I didn't want anything similar to happen to me. I was so impacted by her story that I named one of my daughters after her, Ruth LC. When Ruth died, I made a promise to always be obedient. My sister Ruth's story is one I have taught to all my children. Obedience is better than sacrifice.

Reflection Questions:
1. While reading this story, what lesson did you learn?
2. What is the most significant loss you have experienced and why?
3. What surprised you and why?
4. Could you have made the decision Papa did?

LOSING MY SISTER

"Spend your time celebrating the life versus mourning the death." Joy

My parents had me when they were very young. While they were in love, they had the maturity and insight to know that having a baby didn't equate to marriage. They believed time and growth would allow them to enter this sacred promise with more love and readiness later in life. They married eight years later and remain married.

I guess you could say my father was a lady's man. In 1969, not only was my mom pregnant by my father but another woman was also carrying his child. My sister and I were born thirty-two days apart. I can't imagine what that must have been like for both women. However, if there were issues, I never sensed any conflict or family challenges. Instead, I experienced an inclusive and loving relationship of having a sister by another mother. My mother and Linda, my sister's mother, even became good friends. We were not *half*-sisters, we were whole. They raised us as twins, dressed us alike, and mostly kept us together by having us attend the same schools throughout our formative years.

Shauntel (we called her Shaun) and I never wanted to be apart. Either I was at her house or she was at mine. Although we were polar opposites in many areas, our personalities complemented one another. She was my alter ego. While Shaun was soft spoken and somewhat shy (if she didn't know you), I was outspoken and did the talking for both of us. I had a mild temperament and it took a lot to get me upset while Shaun was a force to be reckoned with if she got angry. All in all, we were each other's protectors.

Throughout our lives, I can only recall us having one argument. We were about thirteen years old and she wanted to walk to the corner store to see her boy crush but I didn't want to go. My grandmother would not allow us to walk alone so Shaun could only go if I agreed to walk with her.

"Joy, will you walk to the store with me? "she asked as I sat on the porch.

"No, I'm reading a book."

"I always go when you want to go. Please!" She begged while combing her hair.

"No, I don't want to go. Stop asking me," I replied, unmoved.

She took a comb and scratched my arm with it. I jumped up from the swing with the intention of hitting her but before I could, she grabbed me and said, "I'm so sorry, please forgive me!"

I stood stunned as I observed the repenting countenance on her face. She then took the comb and scratched her arm as a sign of contrition and solidarity.

"Joy, please forgive me. Don't be mad at me. I'm so sorry. See now my arm looks just like yours."

Up until then, we had never experienced a fight or major disagreement so I was somewhat ill-prepared on how to best deal with what should happen next. So, I decided to ignore her and offer the silent treatment. It worked!

Later that night in bed, she looked at me and said, "Mom said we should never go to bed angry with one other. Please talk to me. I said I was sorry."

I relented and said, "Okay."

"I don't know what I would do if you weren't in my life. When we get older, I hope I never have to bury you. I would be a hot mess. In fact, I think I would be laid out on the floor crying at the funeral."

"Shaun, let's not talk about this. That's sad. I hope I never have to bury you either. Okay, I forgive you now stop being so melodramatic and let's go to sleep."

For our 2012 Christmas vacation, we traveled home to visit my family in Memphis, Tennessee. A tradition was for the Phillips women, which included myself, my mom, my two sisters, and our daughters, to have lunch together without the men. While taking pictures and enjoying the meal, my sister's face looked pain-stricken. Mom inquired and Shaun expressed that her stomach was hurting. She later shared that it had been constant and going on for a couple of weeks. We all encouraged her to go to the doctor to get evaluated. While listening to her, I thought, *something doesn't sound right.*

Several weeks later, after returning to Iowa, Shaun called to tell me that they found a mass in her stomach which needed to be removed. She shared that they thought it might be the big C. She remained hopeful and told me not to worry. I wanted to fly home immediately but she insisted that I stay and take care of the children.

On the day of her surgery, I was scheduled to be out of the country on business but decided to surprise my family and fly home to be there with them. Shaun looked up and saw me as I walked into her hospital room and we both started crying. She was happy to see me and I knew there was no place in the world for me to be other than standing beside her.

After the surgery, I knew something was wrong. My mother's face signaled bad news, however, everyone kept telling me that the surgery went well. Knowing Shaun better than anyone else, I searched her face for signs of what was really going on. She only smiled and said that everything had gone "fine." She also told me it was cancer but she planned to undergo treatment and beat it.

Unfortunately, by that time, Linda was unable to care for Shaun as she was blind and her health was failing. I stayed with my sister for over a week at my parent's house. Even though she was grown, married, and had an eighteen-year-old and a twenty-two-year-old, it was as though we were kids again. We slept side-by-side in our old bed and relived many of our childhood memories.

I took care of her and made sure that she was healing properly. Secretly, I wanted her to tell me how she really felt. I wanted to ask if she was scared but I never did because she never talked about it. She only said, "Let's not watch any hospital shows or anything sad." I understood and complied. During that time, we only had one serious conversation regarding what was happening. One day, she called and asked if I would help with her daughter as she was worried about her and if I would also assist in planning her son's high school graduation party. After agreeing to Shaun's requests, I called my mom to share that it felt like Shaun was telling me, in a roundabout way, that she would not be around much longer.

Months went by and even though my sister was doing great, I still called and checked on her daily because I was worried. She was healing well and responding to the treatments.

The following Labor Day weekend, my parents cooked for the family in Memphis. My mom called to say that she had caught a cold and decided it best for Shaun not to come as she didn't want to compromise her immune system. I agreed. My mom had been trying to reach her all morning but had been unsuccessful. My sister knew that she could not miss my calls as I would hit the roof, so mom asked me to try to reach her.

I dialed her number and it went straight to voicemail. I thought, *that's strange*. I sent a text asking her to call me. She responded that she wasn't feeling well and would rather text. Again, quite unusual. Something in my gut didn't feel right. Over the next couple of hours, we texted back and forth. However, her responses didn't sound like her so I panicked and called my dad to go check on her.

Later, my niece called and said Shaun was extremely sick. Her stomach had swollen so big, it looked as if she was five months pregnant. She was despondent and incapable of speaking. I asked, "Who has been texting me then?" She admitted that my eighteen-year-old nephew had been texting as my sister had informed him to hide what was going on because she knew I would panic. My heart sank.

They rushed Shaun to the hospital where she was immediately admitted into the Intensive Care Unit. The stint in her kidney had been placed incorrectly and had caused an infection that made her entire body septic. I was numb! When I asked if I should come home, everyone said, "NO." The next day, my friend and stylist, Erica, came over with her twin toddlers to provide moral support.

When my mom called and asked to speak to my husband, I immediately fell to the floor because I knew it was bad news. "We will get there as soon as we can," my husband said as he hung up the phone.

As I laid on the flooring wailing in pain, Erika prayed over me. Emotionally, I was losing it and unraveling at the seams. Suddenly, I looked up to find four innocent eyes staring back at me with confusion and fear. Erika's twins were terrified as they didn't understand the magnitude of what was happening. *You're scaring the babies.*

Get up and get yourself together. I gathered myself as best I could and thought only of getting home in time to say goodbye to my sister.

There were only a limited number of outbound flights from Cedar Rapids, Iowa to Memphis, TN and we had already missed the last one of the day. With no other option, we quickly packed a few bags and took the nine-hour drive straight to the hospital.

Once there, the echo of hurried steps followed me as I made my way through the hospital's hallways. Both shoulders slumped from the weight of the moment and my body ached from a place deep within, one that only felt pain and sorrow. My parents came towards me and right as my mom held out her arms, I fell into her body, wailing in sorrow. My mother gently warned me that Shaun was unconscious and would look differently but to hold it together. The doctors advised that she could hear us.

I walked into the room and looked at my sister. Fighting back tears, my internal pain deepened. My mother's words came to me and instead of breaking down, I said, "Okay girl, your hair is a mess. I can't believe they have you looking like this. Let me fix you up." Internally, I smiled because my sister always kept her hair well-groomed and even though we couldn't hear it, I knew she was laughing at my comment. I stood beside my sister, rubbing her face and telling jokes. I shared how much I loved her and asked her to come back to us.

Shaun stayed on life support for seven days. During that time, the doctors told us she was getting worse and there was no chance for recovery or survival. Knowing how close we were, everyone was worried about me but I stayed strong for her two children, her husband, and my parents.

On day seven, my brother-in-law called and said, "Joy, they want to pull the plug on Shaun. What do you think? I can't make this decision alone." With tears in my eyes, I knew it was the decision we needed to make but I couldn't bear to see my sister's life come to an end. How could I watch her take her last breath? I couldn't. My parents went to the hospital and I stayed home with her children and shared the news.

Over the next three years, I struggled with grief. I was depressed and couldn't sleep. Life without her was hard so I poured myself into work, something I could control. Soon, I developed stomach issues. At one point, I was on fourteen pills a day to help digest food. However, the doctors struggled to identify a definitive reason for what was happening.

One day, I went to my gastroenterologist and my daughter Taylor offered to join me. As soon as the doctor came into the exam room, Taylor took over. She told the doctor I was mourning the loss of my sister and she felt nothing else was wrong with me. She even said, "I think this is all in mom's head."

The doctor responded, "I agree. Clinically, nothing is wrong with you. You're grieving and it's manifesting itself in your body in strange ways. I recommend you find a way to deal with the loss and I believe doing so will make all of these symptoms miraculously go away." When we returned home, my daughter threw every bottle of pills I had in the garbage. I called a friend who had dealt with grief and asked for advice.

"Live. You're so afraid of dying that you aren't living. Enjoy your life and celebrate the time you had with your sister. Don't regret her birthday or anniversaries, celebrate them with joy and happiness," she said knowingly.

After hanging up the phone, I said aloud, "Shaun, I miss you. Why didn't you tell me you were going to leave? Why did I have to bury you? I promise to watch out for your children and I promise to LIVE. I promise to celebrate your life and I am going to make sure that I live my life more conscious on how I help heal the world." This is the gift that my beautiful sister gave me. With love and dedication to my best friend and sister, Shaun, you are always and forever in my heart.

Reflection Questions:
1. What reflections do you have after reading this story? What do you need to let go to live?
2. If you have ever lost someone, how do you honor their birthdays or anniversaries? Do you wallow in pain or do you celebrate?
3. What is your greatest fear? How does it manifest in your life?

CHAPTER 4

LOOKING FOR JOY IN RELATIONSHIPS

DIVORCE WAS NEVER A THOUGHT

"If you look for trouble, you most likely will find it." – Ruth

W hen I first entered marriage, I didn't know anything about divorce. Because no one in my family was divorced, I didn't have it as an example. I guess you could say that divorce was never a thought in my mind.

My husband and I were married for fifty-four years. For many, that is a lifetime. It was for me and I was happy. I believe that my attitude and posture relating to marriage kept us together for all those years. I trusted and believed my husband. If he told me something, I took it as truth.

One day he went out with his friends, and didn't come home at his usual time. Interestingly, he didn't come home until the next morning. I was worried as this was out of character for him. When he finally came back, I said, "Where have you been?" He replied, "My car broke down so I just slept in the car under the bridge until I could get help."

Now I know this sounds funny and totally preposterous. However, I chose to believe him and let it go. The next day, I called my sister and began to tell her the story. She was blown away by my husband's account of the night. She said, "Ruth, you are being stupid. You believe everything Johnny tells you!"

I said "Look, this is my husband. I sleep with him every night. Why shouldn't I believe what he said? You weren't there and neither was I. I have no plans to leave him so why make an issue out of it? My bills are paid, and he takes good care of me. Money is not missing, so I choose to take his word and believe him." My sister thought I was crazy. She even referred to me as silly and foolish.

Occasionally during the first few years of our marriage, my sister would tell me that she saw my husband with this person or that person. But I never saw my husband do anything disrespectful to me or our children. But I never looked for anything either. To be able to stay in my marriage, I maintained the mindset of not looking for trouble.

My sister was different. She would look in her husband's pant pockets for any evidence of cheating. She would smell his clothes to see if she could smell perfume. She would even inspect his things looking for lipstick stains. On occasion, she would find something. Then she would be miserable. She would call me crying and sobbing over her marriage. She would temporarily leave him and come to my home only to return to her husband a few days later.

I would often think, why do you look for trouble if you really want to stay? Why leave in the first place if you plan to return? Given that I was happy in my marriage, I never looked for trouble, and I chose to believe my husband. He was mine. I loved him and he loved me. He respected me, took care of me, and was a good husband and father. That's what mattered to me.

Marriage is complicated and there is not a magic rule that will work for every couple. Choose what makes you happy. People may try to tell you things that will make you very unhappy. It's your choice what you choose to believe and receive.

Reflection Questions:

1. What reflections do you have after reading this story? What do you need to let go to live?
2. If you have ever lost someone, how do you honor their birthdays or anniversaries? Do you wallow in pain or do you celebrate?
3. What is your greatest fear? How does it manifest in your life?

I AM NOT MARRIED TO MY MOTHER-IN-LAW

"Marriage is between TWO people! Make sure you are only married to your spouse." Joy

Time and time again, women throughout the years have shared horror stories of a "bad" mother-in-law. The phenomenon is so prevalent that there was even a movie that articulated the role of a mother-in-law as a monster-in-law. This was quite the opposite of the relationship I wanted. When imagining the perfect marriage, I always had a dream to have a great relationship with my mother-in-law. I envisioned us having a special bond. A relationship consisting of her being a prominent and close figure in my life. Let me be clear, I never desired a second mother as I have a mother and I was not in the business of looking for a replacement. So, that's not it. I simply wanted to have a healthy and positive relationship with my mother-in-law.

During my younger years of dating, I would often observe women calling their boyfriend's mother "mom." I thought to myself, *that will never be me*. I will reserve that term for my mother as I wanted to always be clear of her role in my life. Quite frankly, I could never bring myself to use such a significant term so cavalierly.

When I started dating my husband, it was important to meet his family and his parents. I was raised to believe that you can learn a lot about who you are marrying when you understand who they came from and the people who shaped them. I also thought that having a great relationship with my mother-in-law was critical to having a successful marriage.

Growing up, I observed the dynamics and relationship between my mom and paternal grandmother. From my viewpoint, it was great. They were kind, loving, and supportive of one another. My grandmother treated my mom as if she was one of her own. My mom always felt supported by my grandmother when it came to the kids. She was a helper and always desired to keep peace and order in the family. This was the lens in which I defined a mother and mother-in-law relationship.

I remember the first time I met my husband's mother. She was kind, sweet, friendly, loving but always direct in her communication. I instantly fell in love with her. We hit it off from the start. My husband had his own home and frequently I would go to the movies, spend the night, and go out to eat with my soon to be mother-in-law without my husband. In my mind, we had a good relationship.

During our dating years, there was a time in which my husband and I ended the relationship, because I wanted to get married and he wasn't going to let me give him an ultimatum.

My mother-in-law coached me on what to do to "help" my husband come to the right decision in my timeframe. Looking back, I laugh at the conversations she and I had and I remember the wise counsel she offered. The relationship was special. She treated me like a daughter. I just knew that when we got married that we would defy the odds and that my experience would be different than the horror stories I heard from family and friends.

I will never forget the day things changed. It was one of my best and worst days. My husband had proposed and I was on top of the world. The first person I wanted to tell, outside of my parents, was my husband's mother. She deserved to know because she helped me through the process and it worked. I knew she would be overwhelmed with joy because she was the one who repeatedly said her son needed to marry me.

We drove to his mother's home excited, in love, and ready to tell the world. We walked into the house, smiling from ear-to-ear and said, "Guess what? We got engaged!" My mother-in-law stared squarely at both of us and said, "I don't think that is the right thing to do."

Wait a minute, did I hear her correctly? My ears must be deceiving me. I was in shock! What the heck had happened? My husband and I both looked at each other confused. He could see the tears beginning to well up in my eyes.

For the next forty-five minutes, my mother-in-law engaged in a conversation that showed no support for our great news. I was crushed and left the house trembling in tears.

After riding in silence for what felt like hours, my husband pulled over, wiped my tears, and said, "Joy, I told you the first day I met you that you would be my wife. I was just waiting for you to have the same level of confidence that I had that we were soulmates for life. When you marry me, you are not marrying my family or my mother. Their thoughts about you, whether good or bad, will NEVER have an impact on how I feel about you or our marriage. The only person that you need to care about how they feel about you, is me, and I am so in love with you and can't wait to marry you."

In an instant, I was delivered from being bound by what my mother-in-law said, thought, or did. I was free from the mental holds of feeling as though I had to please her or his family. I was released from the bondage of being married to his family. I was liberated to love him and give him the best of me, so that we could make the best of us.

The weight I felt to please his mom was not given to me by him, his mother, or his family. It was a requirement I had given to myself. I'd placed so much emphasis on what she thought about me that I was lacking the focus on the one person that I was marrying, my husband.

How many times have you observed a mother who just loved a girl for her son, but he felt the total opposite? I share this story as encouragement to all the women who feel or felt like I did. Twenty-four years later, I can confirm that my husband meant those words and has lived true to his promise, without fail.

Marriage is hard enough in and of itself. Don't complicate it by trying to be married to anything or anyone other than your spouse. This story is not about my mother-in-law, because I now understand that as a mother, she felt as if she was losing her son and didn't quite know how to articulate her feelings. However, I couldn't let that be my issue.

At the time, the situation was harrowing, but I believe it helped our marriage. My mother-in-law gave me a powerful gift on that day as it created a stable foundation for both me and my husband to know both what and who is most important in our marriage. It created the opportunity for us to design a guardrail around our marriage to prevent anyone or anything from breaking our bond and love for each other. I found solace in knowing that I am not married to my mother-in-law.

I want to encourage every girl or woman to be confident and liberate yourself from the constraints of trying to please anyone other than your spouse. After all this time, we are happy, whole and always put each other first. This is a lesson that I hope inspires others.

Reflection Questions:

1. Have you ever felt pressured to please anyone else other than your spouse in your marriage? If so, who and why?

2. Why have you given power to anyone other than your spouse?

3. If you have given power away, how do you reclaim it?

STICK AND STAY

"Marriage reveals the whole person. The good, bad and sometimes ugly." – Ann

I love my husband dearly and we've been happily married for over 40 years. We were high school sweethearts and dated for seven years before marriage, so you would think that we had all this getting acquainted stuff figured out—at least at the time, I thought we did.

I couldn't wait to get married. I can say that every single day of those seven years we dated, I wanted to marry him. He was it for me and no one else. After being married for a short while, reality set in. It wasn't at all what I thought or imagined it would be.

Marriage reveals the whole person. It reveals the part of us that has been purposely hidden during the dating process because if the other person knew certain things about us, the wedding would be off. People hide secrets such as a hidden child, a hidden past affair, hidden debts, or even hidden vices. They may even hide the fact of not liking some of their soon-to-be in-laws. When dating, we present the polished, mannerly, gentile, well kept, and the overall absolute best, perfect version of ourselves. I always say that you shouldn't marry anyone if you've never seen them angry.

Now I see the person in a totally different light. I see him while he's sleeping, hugging and drooling on the pillow, or he sees that I grind my teeth in my sleep and that I sleep in hair rollers with a scarf tied around my head. Now comes into focus the person who does not hang up clothes, leaves dirty dishes in the sink, doesn't clean out the tub, or clean up behind themselves. Now we see the whole person we married. THIS IS THE REALITY. "A person is who they are when they're not trying to be anyone else."

Did we discuss who's going to cook breakfast, do laundry, or grocery shop? No! From my husband's perspective, it's understood that as the wife, this is my role in the marriage. Nor did we discuss how we were going to share our money or who would pay the bills. I particularly didn't like the fact that I felt like I had to consult with my husband on how to spend "my" money. I now had responsibilities (a lot of them) that I didn't like.

My mom would always say, "Marriage is forever so choose wisely and figure out how to make it work." But the marriage thing was getting the best of me and I wanted out. It was not the fairy tale I had imagined. I wondered, why do people make marriage look so great when in fact, it's such a challenge? Does he want out or is it just me? I often think of this famous Bible verse:

"What therefore God hath joined together, let no man put asunder." (Mark 10:9 KJV)

In hindsight, I now realize my reality was clouded with fear and immaturity. I was afraid and realized that I had it made living at home with Mom and Dad. No responsibilities. My fear was now very real in the form of, I didn't like being married anymore and I wanted to go back home. Oh, did I mention that my Father often told us, "If you ever leave home, you cannot come back."

One day, feeling really upset over something that was petty, I got enough courage to call home and talk to my dad. Thinking he'd feel sorry for me, I began my whining by telling him how I was feeling and that I wanted to leave and come back home. My dad was a man of few words. I guess you could say that he was more of a listener. So, he just listened to me, and when I stopped whining, he asked, "Is that all? Is that everything?" I said, "Yes."

He only said one thing, "Well if things are that bad, I'll come and stay with you until they get better." I was shocked because this is not what I wanted to hear. Totally deflated by his response, after a long pause of silence on the phone, I said, "That's okay, I'll stick and stay." I couldn't imagine my dad coming to live with me. Besides, what would my husband think about all of this? He was none the wiser that I wanted to leave. I never mentioned this to anyone and neither did my dad.

After a while, through my consternation and resolve, I grew and learned several, valuable lessons.

- Marriage is a commitment.
- There is a period of adjustment in marriage.
- Marriage requires hard work.
- Marriage is what you make of it.
- Marriage is not one-sided; it takes two in a marriage.
- If you stick it out, you'll stay married.

Some thirty years later, we celebrated my father's 80th birthday and I shared this story with the audience to honor him. I thanked him for not listening to me or letting me come home. It was because of him that I am currently happily married and that I never left my husband, nor has he left me. When I sat down at the table, beside my father, he said to me, "You know you could've come home if you had really wanted to." I laughed and replied, "Yeah I know because all I had to do was ask Momma."

Reflection Questions:

1. What is your definition of marriage? What are the core elements of a successful marriage?

2. If married, have you ever thought of leaving? If so, why? What made you leave or stay?

3. What were the secrets that you brought into marriage? How have those secrets impacted your relationship? What has been your biggest test in marriage?

4. What made you stick or stay?

A PROMISE TO KEEP

"Be careful what you promise." — Ann

Have you ever agreed to do something thinking you would never have to fulfill the agreement or promise? Have you ever responded out of common courtesy never believing you would actually have to do it? Has there ever been a time when you've been asked, "When I get old, will you take care of me?"

Well, such is my situation. I have an aunt who never married or had children. She lived her life as a loner, allowing only a select few relatives to get close to her. I happened to be one of those select few. She made no secret about how she felt about some of her brothers and sisters, and, at times, treated them quite harshly. If she "liked or cared for you," it was always on her terms.

She was stingy when it came to "her" money. Because she was a hard worker, she had no tolerance for anyone borrowing money or asking for handouts. One of her principles was that no one would borrow her money to pay their bills, after they'd spent their own money having fun or losing it at the casino. She felt people lacked because they didn't know the value of hard work and how to save. She found comfort in judging others based on her values or rules. Her number one rule: Don't ask me for my money. Asking for money was the fastest way to ruin a relationship with her. If you asked for money, she was certain to disconnect and change her opinions about you. The second rule: If you're jobless, you are not eating my food. She despised anyone who would not work. Rule number three: Don't come to visit unless I invite you, because I may not answer the door.

To many in the family, she was just plain mean. In fact, my great aunt referred to her as "that ole devil." She was difficult for most to deal with but, for some reason, she had an affinity to my family. We were the exception to her rule as we got invited to holiday events at her home and remained close throughout the years.

During one of those holiday visits, she looked at me quite casually and said, "You're going to take care of me when I get old...right?" I replied, "Sure. You know I will." Never in a million years did I think that I would be held accountable for that request. No one has a crystal ball to shake and know the future, because if we did, we might make different choices and offer different responses.

Some years later, my aunt's health began to fail as did her mind from dementia. Interestingly, while her memory had failed significantly, she remembered the commitment. She had the hospital call as I had become her power of attorney by that point and it was time for me to make good on my promise. I faced a major crossroads. Never in my wildest dreams did I ever think or were my intentions that I would have to *actually* do what I'd committed to do. *What am I going to do? I work and can't take care of her. Surely someone else can help her. I already have too many commitments. The timing isn't right.* I was conflicted. I loved my aunt despite her ways, but this was a big responsibility. So, I did the only thing I could. I kept my promise.

It has not been easy. My aunt has been in the hospital several times, admitted to the psych ward twice, escaped from one nursing home, resided in an assisted living facility, and is now a contented resident in a secure nursing home facility.

Presently, she is blissfully happy stuck in a time warp with all her joyful memories. I believe she has chosen to forget everything bad that has ever happened in the past. When I visit her, I get to visit the most positive version of her that I have ever known. Mind you, she's talking or rambling on about events that happened in 1945 or 1960 as though it happened today.

There are many things and people she doesn't remember, but the happiness that we share is that she remembers me and that I kept my promise!

Reflection Questions:
1. What promise have you made that you really didn't intend to keep?
2. How do you decline a promise versus being gracious?
3. How would you have responded in this situation? Why?

IF YOU CAN'T BEAT EM'
(The ball is in your court)

"If you can't beat them, you might have more fun joining." Ann

For as long as I can remember, Saturday has been the house cleaning day. We did a bit of straightening up on the other days of the week, but Saturday was different. We changed the linens, cleaned the floors, did laundry…the works! It was all-day cleaning.

When I got married, nothing changed. Saturday was still cleaning day. I soon realized that I was the only one doing all the cleaning, while my husband would go to the den, sit on the sofa, and watch wrestling and college football all day. Sunday was more of the same minus the wrestling and with professional football instead of college. I can't count how many times I asked, coaxed, invited, or even demanded that he get up and help me clean.

One Saturday in particular, I thought to myself, *I'll fix him.* I got up earlier than he did and removed the electrical cord from the rear of the floor model television. It didn't take him long to figure out what I'd done. Needless to say, this made him quite angry. After realizing it wouldn't change anything, I relented and gave him the cord. He resumed his normal Saturday activity of sitting in front of the television, doing nothing. By that point, I was boiling with anger. We shared a few choice words, but I remember saying to him, "If you're going to sit here all day, doing nothing and watching television, so am I." And so, it began.

I really couldn't stomach the wrestling, which I call "grown man's cartoons", but my stubbornness wouldn't let me move. I sat and watched. However, when it came to football, I was intrigued. I asked my husband questions about the game, trying to understand. I could tell this was really irritating him (which I didn't mind). He ignored me, probably thinking and silently praying I'd lose my resolve and leave him alone. That was not happening!

I bought a book about football and soon learned the game, referee hand signals, rules, teams, coaches, conferences, and star players. I bought a subscription to *Sports Illustrated* as a Father's Day gift for my husband, but had it sent to my office so I could read it first. Adding to his irritation, I would often bring home the magazines and suggest stories I thought he should read. I soon realized that I thoroughly enjoyed football and it was exciting. Saturday now transcended into a weekly sports viewing event at my home. We'd sit and watch football. Saturday football grew into Monday night football, the playoffs, and the Super Bowl. I became a walking book on football stats and players. My coworkers even bought me a sports trivia book as a Christmas gift. How many women know who Y.A. Tittle is or the college that Dan Marino attended?

So, you might ask, what happened to the Saturday chores? Well, that is one of the advantages of having daughters. The tasks of the house became the chores for the children. Just know, they did their part, but I still came through and made things look like I wanted. However, I would do the chores with the television tuned loudly through the house so I didn't miss any big moment.

Now I've broadened my knowledge and enjoyment of sports to include college and professional basketball. One year, I talked my husband into buying season college football tickets, season college basketball tickets, and season pro NBA tickets. This was total insanity. There was no way we could attend all the games, but it was fun trying, and we did! We had outfits and decorations; this was our fun times together. I think I became more of a sports fan than him.

Loving and knowing sports became an asset. Professionally, it helped me to become a better communicator. Talking about sports is an easier, more comfortable conversation in male-dominated settings as opposed to talking about politics, religion, or current events. It allowed and afforded me opportunities to have relaxed, ice-breaker conversations in meetings with male managers and counterparts.

Think about it, most sports fans display their love of sports in hats, shirts, team logos, and the like. It's effortless to strike up a conversation with a stranger when he's wearing a Duke cap, because you know he follows the team. Ironically, it surprises and disarms most men to have a woman know and discuss sports so confidently. I had one gentleman tell me that he envied my husband to have the perfect wife like me who loved sports. Little did he know, this story started out as a "Goal Line Stand" with no movement on either side!

Reflection Questions:
1. What are your weekend rituals, and do they provide an opportunity for you to enjoy hobbies or pleasures?
2. Are you a sports fan? If so, how did you fall in love with sports?
3. What hobby does your spouse have that you could benefit from joining?
4. What might be the advantages of trying something that your spouse enjoys?

AN UNSTUFFED TEDDY BEAR

"Avoid unfulfilling relationships as if they were the plague." - Taylor

"Girl you're too picky. You'll never find someone to treat you like that. You're asking for a lot from a guy." LIES YOU TELL! I wish I had a dollar for every time one of my friends tried to give me "good advice." One of the most important lessons I learned about dating is not to rely 100% on anyone's perspective or guidance.

You have your miserable friends, lonely friends, fake friends, best friends, etc. Then there's your good ole family. You have the nosey ones, protective ones, the ones that mean well, and the ones who want to control your life. Between the combination of friends and family, you have a peanut gallery you never asked for. Relying too heavily on others' advice landed me in some of life's best and worst circumstances. Let's start with the worst. I was a junior in college and my longtime boyfriend and I had broken up. Throughout college, I'd had the same boyfriend and now I was ready to date and see what else was out there. Truthfully, I was hurt by the breakup and was looking for someone completely opposite of him. That was mistake number one. Just because my situation changed did not mean my values needed to change, a lesson I learned quickly. Not to mention, everyone had an opinion regarding the relationship. I can sum up my time with the new guy in three words—unstuffed teddy bear.

He actually bought me an unstuffed teddy bear as a gift. Nope, there was nothing inside. Listening to my friends and ignoring my gut landed me with an unstuffed teddy bear relationship. The key is knowing what advice to take, what advice to ignore, and what expectations are non-negotiable.

Deep down, I knew things wouldn't work. Unfortunately, listening to pieces of myself and the biased advice of many, caused me to sacrifice my standards. I went for someone entirely different with new qualities versus looking for someone new with the same attributes I cherished in past relationships. Despite Mr. Unstuffed Teddy Bear, I have no regrets. I'm thankful to have learned the lesson as a young adult as some people don't find clarity until after they've walked down the aisle.

I've learned that advice is just that, advice. It's not fact nor fiction. Once I let that sink in, I realized I was relying on someone else's opinion about MY life and allowing their opinions to dictate my decisions. People shouldn't know all your business and there's no way they can make a diagnosis without your full chart.

I've learned that there are people who want you to be miserable right along with them. Mainly I've learned to listen, hear it, decide what advice I want to take, and keep my business to myself. You must choose who you date based on your standards, not other people's standards. "Girl he's a great guy." According to whose standards, mine or yours? My standards are very clear: Christian, respectful, attractive, proactive in life goals, intelligent, etc. You should never lower your standards or settle for anyone based on the opinions or well-intended advice/help of others. If you do, you might find yourself with an unstuffed teddy bear. If you don't know what your standards are, you probably aren't ready to date or need to take a break to self-reflect.

I'm no expert, but I know where I have made the right turns and where I have erred. Bits and pieces of knowledge from everyone serves a purpose. For instance, my great great-grandmother's perception of dating and marriage is valid but different than my mother's advice and experiences dating. Balancing different points of view and being confident in my own intuition has been key in dating.

Reflection Questions:

1. Have you ever had an unstuffed bear relationship? Why was it unstuffed?

2. What are your non-negotiable relationship standards?

3. What advice have you received that left you unstuffed?

CHAPTER 5

OBTAINING JOY IN SUCCESS

IT'S NOT PERSONAL

"An angry person can't think." -Ann

Early in my career, I learned a valuable lesson that became a thread in the fabric of my life. I attended a meeting with an area sales manager to discuss budgets and how my staff could support his sales team to meet their goals. This manager had a reputation of being difficult to deal with but was well respected because he was an achiever and his district was always at the top in sales performance. I can't say that I disliked him, but he was certainly someone that I found intimidating. From the moment we entered and closed the meeting room door, I could sense from his demeanor the he was not pleased about something. He didn't ask me any questions, nor was he interested in hearing my thoughts regarding the matter at hand. This so-called meeting was nothing more than an all-out "butt chewing", scolding and yelling session.

Shocked, chagrined and hurt at the manner in which this man had spoken to me, I wanted nothing more than to get up and leave. The meeting was so contentious that I became non-verbal and unresponsive. At this point

I'm losing it because I'm no longer hurt, but now I'm really angry with all kinds of mean thoughts rolling around in my head about this vile man. I really wanted to unload and tell him what I really thought about him!

Nearing the verge of tears and an emotional meltdown, I kept repeating the mantra over in my mind, *I will not cry. I can't let him see me cry.* I was totally caught off guard at his insensitivity and audacity. I can't say how long the meeting lasted, because although I was still sitting in the chair, mentally I had checked out five minutes into the meeting. When he completed his meeting agenda, feeling very proud of himself, he smirked and said, "Let's go to lunch."

What? I nearly fell out of my chair. Did he just ask me to go to lunch? Does he not understand or sense the loathing I currently feel for him, not even wanting to be in his presence, let alone go to lunch with him? I respectfully declined.

His entire temperament changed. He leaned forward, thoughtfully considering his words before he spoke.

"Come on now, I will not allow you to sit here and be angry with me about this. What we discussed was business and not about you. **It's not personal Ann.** Keep the two separate. You became emotional, taking it personal, and losing all sense of focus and purpose. Nothing we discussed was a personal indictment of you. In fact, I like you! In order to be a successful manager, you need to learn how to separate your emotions from business."

Not wanting to appear unprofessional or petty, I put aside my feelings and went to lunch. Although I can't say it was enjoyable, it was pleasant.

I gave this experience a lot of thought, consideration and self-evaluation for some months. Truthfully, I was embarrassed and felt demeaned. What I came away with was a clear path of how and who I wanted to be. I learned that I did not want to be a manager that was inconsiderate, disrespectful and an abuser of authority and power, because I knew how it felt to be on the receiving end of a tirade. I also learned that sometimes the message can get so obscured or lost because of the delivery (yelling and screaming) of the messenger. My resolve was that I would practice the "Platinum Rule" and always treat people the way "they" want to be treated...personally and professionally.

I recalled the words a wise person, my husband, once told me, "An angry person can't think, and a thinking person can't be angry. At the very moment a person makes you angry, that person has taken control of the situation and of you, because you're not thinking...but reacting."

Reflection Questions:

1. What are your "hot buttons" in business settings? Why?

2. How do you deal with anger? What might be a better way?

3. How do others experience you when you are angry?

MY LITTLE BECAME MUCH

"Take whatever you have been given in life and make MUCH… that is the true definition of wealth."– Ruth

Happiness is the collective sum of all things family. I used to always say, "If I make my family happy, then I'll be happy." I never desired to have fame, fortune, or luxurious things. I was far from interested in diamonds or furs or anything material.

My husband was a hard worker throughout his life. All four of our children attended college and we learned early in life to make do with what we had. My husband lived for eighty-four years and during his entire lifetime, he never earned more than $250 a week. Yes, you heard me right, $250 a week. However, my children and I never wanted for anything. We always had food, clothes, shelter, and many of the things in life we desired. We bought a home, because we wanted to have ownership of something to leave our children. Our bills were always paid on time and we didn't borrow from others. In fact, we were the lenders to many of our siblings and family members. By all accounts of poverty and wealth, we should have been considered poor, but we were not. We were rich in love and in my mind, we had everything because we had each other.

We had a FAMILY.

As I reflect over my life, I believe our little became much, because I managed my home with the mindset that my family was the greatest gift I had been given as a woman. I lived by this biblical truth, *"Every wise woman buildeth her house: but the foolish plucketh it down with her hands"* (Proverbs 14.1 KJV). God gave me the strength and wisdom to be able to guide our home at a young age with the little we had been given to ensure that our children had a successful and happy life.

I once read the following story:

There was a rich man and a poor man. The rich man could buy anything he wanted as he had wealth beyond measure. Likewise, he was very kind and gracious to the poor man. Because of his kindness, the poor man wanted to do something for the rich man to show his gratitude. However, when the poor man visited his home, he felt inadequate to give back because of all the expensive things he observed. He looked at the rich man and said, "I have nothing to give you, but if you ever need me, I am here. If you ever lose everything, I can teach you how to live and survive with little."

The moral of the story is that both had a treasure. The rich man's treasure was his wealth and riches. The poor man's treasure was his strategic ability to take the little he had and make much. That is how I view my life. I have never had much as it related to wealth or money, but I have always been rich in spirit and love. It has been my most significant accomplishment to share this treasure with my greatest gift, my family.

Reflection Questions:
1. What parts of this story could you connect with and why?
2. What is your greatest treasure and why?
3. Have you ever thought, my life would be so much better if I had more money? If so, how are you making wealth with what you have?

THE MOVE

"Growth comes from discomfort." -Taylor

"Taylor! Tyron! Mom and dad have some news that we need to share with you." Maybe we were getting a dog, or maybe a cat! My mind ran with ideas and I was excited and hopeful for the news. But as I stood before them, their heads hung low avoiding eye contact. Based upon the looks on their faces, this surprise was going to be unforgettable. After what felt like hours, my mother blurted out, "We're moving to Iowa."

You know that numbness you feel when you've laid on your arm too long? My body felt that way. I didn't say anything because I was too full of emotions. Somehow, I knew it was not the time for tears. My brother looked up at me puzzled and longing for understanding. For the first time, I couldn't provide him with an explanation.

I never envisioned myself living anywhere other than Memphis. My first thought was to ask the reason behind the decision. We were a happy family that attended church every Sunday and had future plans in that community already. I was an academic scholar, my brother was starting basketball at Upward, and my dad was his coach.

Why fix something that was not broken? I didn't have the answers. I could have asked but it was pointless. No matter how angry, sad, and confused I was, in two months my family would be moving. I would no longer be a resident of 1369 Trail Run Lane. Everything that I was taught to memorize and cherish would now be insignificant. Our home would be empty and lifeless without the laughter of our voices to fill it. I tried to imagine another family in my house; the thought was too piercing. "New beginnings are exciting," my mother reminded me, yet I was not excited; I was terrified. I didn't even know where Iowa was located on the map. It sounded like one of those barren states no one ever mentioned.

My night was restless. I tossed and turned for hours as I waited to wake up from this never-ending nightmare. In times like these, faith was my stronghold, my safe place upon which I heavily relied. My eyes stared up at the ceiling waiting for a voice, waiting for God to assure me of my fears and doubts.

Questions without answers were all I could think about. *What am I going to say at school tomorrow? What am I going to tell my friends? Do I even try on my homework and quiz assignments? Does anyone know where Iowa is? I am still not sure where Iowa is located,* I thought. It was then, in the solitude of my room and confinement, that I shed my first tears. The chill of the wet droplets on my pillow gave me comfort. With every tear, I drifted closer and closer to sleep and my mind was finally at rest.

The sweet aroma of eggs and bacon woke me from my slumber and I raced to the kitchen table. Family breakfast was usually only on Sundays, so this was an unexpected delight. Lucky for me, I was in no rush to get ready for school. The chimes of the doorbell rang and I knew it was Symone. We rode to school together every morning. Symone and I had been best friends since diapers and we were hinged at the hip. She always felt more like a sister than just a friend. Telling her about the move would crush her but I wanted her to be the first one to know. I couldn't take the pressure of this secret for much longer. I decided to blurt it out.

"Symone, we are moving to Iowa."

"Tay, stop playing," she said as she laughed.

She soon recognized my silence as assurance and the expression on her face shifted. Suddenly, two arms were wrapped around me so tightly I could not breathe. Her caress made me feel guilty. I was deserting someone who needed me. We were intoxicated with fear of our upcoming separation.

Two weeks later, it was time for my annual birthday party and sleepover with all my friends. Decorations were bought, cupcakes were frosted with love, and the invitations were sent out. Birthday parties were always a special event. However, it was imperative that this party be perfect. It was also my going-away party and last chance to spend with the only friends I had known.

I pasted a smile on my face as I waited near the door for my guests to arrive. Pink streamers dangled high from the ceiling, giving me nausea. Finally, my first guest arrived giving me something to do. Everyone came dressed ready for the model photo shoot we had planned. Our lips were coated with the pasty brick red lipstick, powder was gently brushed on our smooth baby-like skin, and pink passion nail polish adorned our nails. Soon, we were flawless and camera ready.

After pretending to be models and embracing my inner Tyra Banks (we share the same birthday), it was time to open gifts and cut the cake. The beautifully decorated pile of presents did not excite me. I opened and carefully read each card written and given by my friends. Who knew saying goodbye would be so complicated? I felt special and lucky to have friends who cared for me so much. Minute by minute, I held back tears fighting to escape my eyes. As I unwrapped each gift with reluctant praise, I came closer and closer to breaking down emotionally. I would miss their faces and the friendships we shared.

"Happy Birthday to You, Happy Birthday to You..." They began to sing the birthday song as I admired the cake which displayed my favorite colors. The red and orange light from the candles sparkled as my mother continued to light them. Thirteen candles were lit to symbolize my years on earth. Years that felt like a waste. Blowing out the candles would signify an end to my past.

"Taylor, honey, make a wish," my mom prompted. All I wanted was to stay in that moment with my friends.

The move was one of the hardest transitions in my life. I did not understand it and believed it to be unfair. As I closed my eyes, I wished that my future would once again bring me a HAPPY birthday with friends I loved.

Reflection Questions:
1. What is the most significant change or challenge you've faced in life?
2. What part of this story could you identify with?
3. How do you deal with change?

LESSONS FROM A FATHER

*"Don't let **anything** rule you, you rule it. You should always stay in control of the situation."-*
Charity

My father, Monroe King, was a great man and I loved him dearly. I loved to hear him sing and talk about his upbringing. He would share stories about his siblings and parents, but he spoke very little about his father, who left him when he was thirteen years old.

Sitting on his knee, he would sing song after song. Even today, I remember some of the songs he sang to me. My father was great with his hands. I guess you could say in my opinion, he was great at everything. He was a man of many talents and loved his family. He built the log cabin in which we lived. It's hard to imagine now but we all lived in one room.

My father taught us to take care of our bodies. In many regards, he was our doctor. We didn't have much access to hospitals or nurses, so we had to rely on what we were taught. He would say, "Don't eat too much. Hard work doesn't hurt nobody if they are well fed, and they don't strain." He made sure to tell young girls and women never to strain their bodies. He believed girls' insides were delicate and required special care.

He taught us to keep something on our heads at all times when it was cold. He would say, "Keep your chest covered and put something on your feet." When it was hot, he would put jimson leaves in the top of our hats to keep us cool. He would also use the leaves to "break" any fever. It worked. There weren't any doctors close to our home, so my father would go to the woods and gather herbs to keep us healthy. He had so many remedies and concoctions to use whenever we got sick. I guess it worked. I am 100 years old and I have never had one surgery. Here are some of the herbs and remedies he used:

Jimson—fever
Horehound—cough
Catnip—baby hives
Cow chip tea—flu
Penny rye—fleas

My father was well respected in our neighborhood by both Blacks and Whites. He was an advocate for doing what was right and he helped many Black people by speaking up for them. He was charismatic and a great speaker; for some reason, White men listened to him. Whenever he was in the company of a man (Black or White), he referred to them as gentleman. He was intentional as he wanted them to behave gentle as a man.

He was a leader and a voice of peace. He would come home and tell us stories of how he kept Black people from being beaten. One day, he shared a story in which the White man was going to punish a Black man by beating him with an axe handle. Unfortunately, that was how Blacks were treated, inhumane. My dad spoke to the White man and asked him to have mercy on the man. He continued to talk to him until he decided to surrender and take his advice. My dad was a powerful influencer and force of strength. He knew how to stay in control and not lose his temper.

He was a prophet. He preached to the White people just like he did the Black. He told them Jesus was soon to come, not just one day but every day. He instilled in us the importance of Sundays. On Sundays, no one was allowed to work. Sunday's dinner had to be cooked on Saturday. We did everything needed to be done before Sunday. We went to church and learned about the Bible. He taught us to love and be proud of who we were. We were born from great leaders and we too needed to stand up and lead.

Reflection Questions:
1. What stories do you remember growing up? How have they influenced you?
2. What is a favorite memory of your father? Or mother?
3. How you ever had to take an herb or concoction as a child to get well? If so, what?

CHAPTER 6

JOY IN DISCOVERY

I LOST ME

"Every woman deserves "me" time. It's needed,
necessary, and fundamental to your happiness."
— Joy

Have you ever felt lost? One day I was sitting on the couch watching a self-help show with my husband. A woman shared that at one point in her marriage, she felt as though she had lost herself. My husband looked perplexed and said, "Wow, that must be awful. How can you lose yourself? Babe, I am so glad that you never felt that way."

"I lost me at one point," I said.

"Joy, you are going to have to help me understand. This is hard for me to believe and I certainly don't understand how you *lost* yourself? When did this happen and how did I miss it?" I then shared my story with him.

Early in our marriage, I was very excited to be a wife and even happier to be a mother. In my mind, I was living the dream. I had a great husband and two amazing children—I had it all. I was happy, felt loved, supported, and appreciated by my husband and family.

Then one day, I remember waking up and feeling sad. My daughter was five and my son was two at the time. I started revisiting my life. Every day, I made decisions that were centered around my husband, children, job, and church. And, each time I had a baby, I reinvented myself by changing a physical feature, such as my hair, clothes, or style. It was as if I needed to revalidate who I was. Or maybe, I was just trying to feel good about my new self-image. To be honest, I had weight to lose after each pregnancy and don't forget the permanent change of shoe size or the wonderful stretch marks that invade your body. But I should still feel sexy, right? Instead, I was sad and guilty for feeling that way because, didn't I have it all?

One day, the kids were gone, my husband was at work, and I was home alone, a rarity. As I sat in bed, I pondered, *what do I want to do?* I couldn't figure out how to process the thought because for the last seven to eight years, I'd felt invisible. Wow…that was scary to actually admit.

I felt invisible as it related to my needs, wants, and desires. My entire way of thinking had dramatically changed since I got married. Imagine living a life in which every decision you make is with someone else in mind. Where you rarely think about yourself first. Even simple things like what we would eat for dinner was never about me. I always considered what my husband liked or what the children wanted to eat. Sadly, my style and dress had changed.

When I shopped, I would come home and share my wardrobe purchases with my husband. If he wasn't particularly fond of an item, I would return it. Not because he'd asked me to, because I wanted him to approve and like my clothes. Again, nothing I did was for me. It was as if I needed someone else's confirmation to feel good about who I was.

Each time I walked into a department store, I would immediately visit the children's area. Once done, I would visit the men's department. Then if I had time or money left, I would go to the home area. I rarely went to the women's department; that was the last thought on my mind. One day, while shopping with my mom, she said, "What do you ever purchase for yourself?" I didn't have an answer.

Simple things such as my daily schedule was planned around the children. I wanted to make sure I was not out while the kids were tired or sleepy. Even if I had plans, I would forego them and head home if they fell asleep. They dictated my life.

On that day, I cried as I sat in bed struggling to figure out what I would do all alone. I felt lost. It was no one's fault but mine. I had allowed my circumstance. The self-depleting process in which little by little, I'd given up my power and unique identity. I was not Joy; I was Mrs. Fitzgerald, a wife and mother of two.

After I cried, I got angry. I was upset with myself for creating my own invisibility. I had given up career decisions for my children so that I could be as present as possible in their lives. Frustrated, I picked up the phone and called my mom and asked, "Have you ever felt like you lost yourself?"

Because I never remembered any women in the family having this conversation, I naturally assumed it was an issue reserved only for me. My mom laughed and said, "Absolutely." It was the most freeing and liberating answer she could have given me.

"Joy, women are givers. They are nurturers. We give and give up so much of ourselves that we sometimes forget to give TO OURSELVES. Baby, you can only take 100 from 100. When it is all gone, you have zero. You must be thinking about how you recharge and reenergize so that you can be a great wife and mom and, most importantly, a GREAT version of Joy. This requires prioritizing your needs at times."

"Mom, how do I do that? Where do I even start?"

"First of all, find something in your life that is just about you. Something that you enjoy and makes you feel good and isn't in any way attached to your husband or children. It needs to be yours. It must be something you look forward to doing. Secondly, being a working mom is hard. But it is also rewarding if done well. Every time you get paid, reward yourself. It could be something as simple as buying yourself a pair of pantyhose. You need to feel like what you are doing has a personal payoff for you. Trust me. It works!"

That day, I committed to "finding Joy." I loved to read and I also loved girlfriend time so I called three of my closest friends and asked if they would be interested in starting a book club with me. They loved the idea and agreed to help.

The book club was the beginning of restoring things back into my life as an adult mom and wife. Sister to Sister Book Club, because the women and I created a sisterly bond, was the best thing I could have done for myself. We laughed, cried, and shared stories along with girly advice. It was therapeutic; it was healing.

I also took my mom's advice and rewarded myself every paycheck with a small item. Whether it was a skirt or a new hair product, I was consistent. The ritual forced me to think about my wants and needs.

I love my children and husband. But, I realized to be the best wife and mom, I needed to prioritize myself. I am so thankful that I found ME!

Reflection Questions:
1. If this story resonated with you, please describe why or why not?
2. If you have ever felt lost, how did you go about finding yourself?
3. If you currently feel lost, what is contributing to this feeling? What do you need to start, stop or continue to help provide greater clarity and self-worth in your life?
4. Are you happy? Why or why not?

MOM, I NEED BIRTH CONTROL

"Your children should be comfortable with you when it matters most." – Taylor

"Mom, I think I need to take birth control." Let that sink in for a moment. At the ripe age of nineteen, I said that to my mother. In my circle of friends, I think I might have been the last one to have that conversation. Women have various reasons for needing the pink pill wheel: cramps, pregnancy prevention, migraines, etc. My reasons were obviously not apparent by the look on my mom's face. She was looking at me like she wanted to say, "Excuse me, take a seat, and let's have the sex talk all over again."

Our first discussion about sex entailed her saying, "Look, don't be out here sucking any lil' boys' private parts. That's all I want to say about this as I know school teaches you the rest." Given that "talk," you should understand why I was reluctant to go down that road again. Plus, I was a nineteen-year-old virgin with the diary to prove it. However, sex had nothing to do with my need for birth control.

Since I was about fifteen, I've had bothersome periods. I would miss school and work because of the excessive pain from cramps. Feeling like knives were ripping through my uterus is an understatement. I dreaded my time of the month and according to the doctor, getting on the pill was the best solution. The doctor told me it would also help with my migraines. AWESOME! HELLO! It would alleviate not one, but two, of my problems. Order me some right now! But first, I had to talk to Joy (that's how I refer to her when she's not around).

You might wonder why I mentioned it to her at all since I was already nineteen and did not need her permission. I had access to my own insurance, doctor, and money. But the thing was, I was not looking for her permission. I wanted my mother's advice and guidance. The fact that I felt comfortable talking to her about any topic is something I cherish. Many of my girlfriends have made simple mistakes because they didn't feel like they could discuss things with their mothers.

Ultimately, I am glad I spoke to my mother about getting on the pill because after we got past the fact that I didn't need it for sex (even though I still don't think she believed me), she informed me of all the problems she had with birth control. In my family, we have a history of fibrocystic breasts. That means a lot of things, but for my purposes, it meant that any extra estrogen in my body could cause cysts. That detail was something my mother knew about my family but my doctor did not. Despite what she told me, I weighed the pros and cons and decided easier periods were worth it, especially since I didn't even know if I had fibrocystic breasts. *Later I learned that I did, read, "The C Word," to learn more about my journey.*

Having conversations about health and personal matters with parents can sometimes be difficult but it is crucial for parents to provide the ease, comfort, and safety for their children to share personal and private concerns. Thankfully, I have that type of relationship with my mother and both me and my brother feel that we can talk to our parents about anything. While it may be embarrassing and uncomfortable, on both sides, they have told us that we can tell them anything. Although they may not like some of the things we might share, we value their opinion and know they will always have our best interests at heart. I encourage all moms and dads to talk to your children. There may be serious things going on with their health and if you don't give them a safe space to share, you will never know.

Reflection Questions:

1. Did you share any personal stories with your parents? Why or why not?
2. If you have children, what level of comfort or safety have you provided for them to talk to you about private matters?
3. How can you ensure that you are a trusted source and that you don't make them feel judged?

I'M NOT WONDER WOMAN

"Wonder Woman is not real so don't be afraid to ask for help!" - Ann

It's 5 a.m. and time for me to get up, or shall I say, get my day started. I go to the girls' bedrooms and peep in on them as they sleep just to ensure they're okay. I shower and get dressed, prepare an on-the-go breakfast, and prepare lunches. Next, I pack the baby's diaper bag and wash a few dishes left from the night before.

My toughest job of the morning is literally pulling my oldest daughter out of bed to start the difficult task of trying to keep her awake, so she can wash her face and brush her teeth. Most mornings, she's walking and talking with her eyes closed while I comb her hair and dress her for school. I gather up her backpack and lead her to the car so I can drop her off at my mom's house for school. Fortunately, she can walk to school because it's right around the corner from my parent's house.

After dropping off my daughter, I return home where my husband is now awake and preparing for work. I get the baby a bottle ready, because I know she'll be awake soon and ready to eat. I start packing the car with the baby's diaper bag and my briefcase. I get the baby up and give her the bottle hoping she'll fall back asleep as I load her into the car seat and head across town to the babysitter's house who, thank God, is my mother-in-law. Now it's 7:30 a.m., and I'm finally on my way to work. I arrive by 8 a.m.

After a stressful day at work, it's finally 5 p.m., and I do my morning routine in reverse—pick up the baby, grab my daughter, and head home. When we arrive home, it's 6:30 p.m. Within thirty minutes, my husband asks, "What's for dinner?" WHAT? I can't believe he fixed his mouth to ask me that. I fume with anger. He's been home two hours and is waiting for me to fix him dinner after all I've have to do. I hold my tongue and don't speak the awful thoughts that are infiltrating my mind and instead, proceed to settle the girls and get dinner started.

Later that night, while everyone is asleep, I call my mother and begin to share my frustrations of feeling overwhelmed with too many responsibilities and no help from my spouse. She asks, "Why don't you ask him to help you?" Suddenly it dawns on me. I had never asked my husband to help with the girls or with anything I considered as my wife or motherly duties. I was an independent woman and felt it was my job to do everything that involved the children, while at the same time I was unjustifiably feeling anger towards him for being inconsiderate by not helping me, when all I had to do was ask for his help.

When I discussed my frustration with my husband, responsibilities quickly changed around the house. I told him I needed his help. Thankfully, he was more than willing and happy to be needed and feel like an integral part of the family. He volunteered to drop off and pick up the baby, because it also gave him the opportunity to visit his parents. At first, he was not versed in cooking but did his best to pitch in by trial and error. Soon he became a proficient cook and enjoyed being creative in the kitchen.

The experience taught me a multitude of lessons with the first being, "no man is an island." We all need help every now and then and if you allow, some people will be content sitting on the sidelines and watching you work. With childhood stories and movies like "Wonder Woman," creating unrealistic expectations for women, we fall into the trap of trying to be and do everything for everyone. Most importantly I learned, don't expect people to read your mind or assume they already know how you feel or what you need. No, they don't know. You need to ASK and REQUIRE!

Reflection Questions:

1. What demands have you placed on yourself that seem overwhelming? Have you ever stopped and asked for help? Why or why not?

2. What are the things in life that give you energy? What takes away your energy? Why?

3. What requirements or definitions of success were part of your upbringing that have shaped who you are today? Do you need to reject any of those teachings? If so, which ones and why?

OUT OF THE BOX

"You don't have to fit in a box."- Taylor

Have you ever met a nerdy child who asks their parents to create assignments throughout the summer so that they can feel like they are still in school? What about the child who gets excited about school supplies? Or maybe a child who gets overjoyed to start another new school year, because they love learning? That was and forever will be me.

My college graduation will take place in a few weeks and I still feel like that elementary school child who didn't want to leave school. School and education have always been an important part of my life but second grade changed the game. My second-grade teacher, Mrs. Mullins, stretched a muscle that many teachers do not— the ideation muscle. Most of the time, school is black and white in that you either have the right or the wrong answer. Mrs. Mullins lived in the grey but still made it clear that math was the only absolute in her classroom. Not everything has an answer, even in science. She was my first teacher that only taught one subject, the subject of learning.

She was known as tough on academics but always managed to turn a wrong answer into a valuable lesson and not just a bad grade; she was an educator, not just a teacher. She was my trailblazer into a whole new world of learning. For those reasons, I dreaded the last day of second grade. Her personal attachment and desire to mold each and every student has been invaluable in my life. I didn't want to leave Mrs. Mullins class.

I remember being told it was time to line up for the car rider's line. Immediately, I began to cry as I knew this was a goodbye I didn't want to say. I cried so hard, the principal of the school, along with Mrs. Mullins, consoled me. They both grabbed one of my arms and helped walk me to my mom's car. I looked up and they were teary-eyed too. We were a mess. No, I was a mess.

Why was I a mess? Admittedly, I am a little dramatic. The real issue was that I classify myself as a dabbler/divergent. I love all subjects and exploring different areas of thought which is inherent in school. However, at some point along your educational journey, they want to put you in a box. Webster's dictionary defines a box as a rectangular container made up of straight lines. Kids are even taught to only color inside the lines. Growing up as a child, as early as I can remember, family members often asked, "What do you want to be when you grow up?" In my family, if you didn't have an answer, they would give you one. That is the beginning of the box. By asking the question, they are signaling that you must have a defined plan in life as discovery is certainly not an option.

Even in college, they try to put you in a box. Where's the box for people who don't want one? Why does there have to be a box? Where is my box? What if I can't find my box? But everyone keeps telling me I need a box. Sometimes it feels like success is tied to choosing the "right" box. To some degree, I often wondered if I was missing the mark because I didn't have the answer to many of those bigger questions. My approach to life was not a rectangle shape made up of straight lines. Instead, my life approach had more squiggly lines and often produced an unfinished, irregular shape. I would sometimes ask my mom, "Is it strange that I don't know what I want to do in life?" Because all my friends appeared to have confident answers and a greater sense of direction, it felt as though I was missing something.

What I craved was to *dabble*. I guess the closest people can get to this box is having a new role every few years, if they're lucky. That's why I love school. It gives you the time to dabble. But I won't lie, in the past four years, I probably enjoyed the college part more than the school part. Wink, Wink.

On a serious note, school keeps you occupied in a routine. You know your schedule, your teachers, you get syllabi for the whole year, and there aren't many surprises. It allows you to dabble and learn new things, maybe to even help you "find" your box.

Maybe this is why I liked school so much. However, there is no syllabus for the real world. You have to wake up and figure it out. Summer days full of uncertainty and ambiguity are not as appealing. In college, if a class becomes too challenging, you have the option to drop it. In contrast, there's only one way to drop out of real life, and for me that is NOT an option. The reality of a lost safety net is unsettling to some people. But guess what? That dreaded last day is coming and this time, I won't have to be dragged off campus by my professors. Education is always available no matter your age, circumstance, or ability. I know this is my last day of undergraduate school, but it certainly is not my last day of school as I still don't have a box. I'm also proud to say that I don't want a box.

I encourage anyone reading this, if you're in a box, expand it. Basically, do not allow life or anyone to put limits or contain you. Give yourself permission to dabble and learn. If you are in search of a box, take your time. It's okay. If you are none of the above, then be out of the box. That's my current state of mind and where I have found joy — OUT OF THE BOX!

Reflection Questions:
1. What activities do you engage in on a regular basis to learn and grow?
2. Have you ever considered yourself a dabbler? If so, why?
3. Are you in a box, out of the box or trying to find a box? And why?

MOM, I HAVE A BEAD IN MY NOSE

"Winning in life is an individual sport." -Joy

E ven as a child, I had a strong desire to win. During the first week of kindergarten, I met my best friend, Laverne. We were both happy, loving, five-year-olds excited to be in school. One day, I wore a green beaded necklace, thinking I was really dressed up. When I got to the locker, I showed Laverne my necklace. She grabbed it for a closer look and it accidentally broke. Green beads dispersed all over the floor. We hurriedly picked up the beads before anyone noticed.

Laverne then took two beads and stuck them up her nose saying, "Look at me. I can stick two beads up my nose. I bet you can't!" Overflowing with the competitive spirit, I responded, "Well, I can beat you and stick three beads up my nose!" After I followed through with the bright idea to stick three beads up my nose, I tried to get them out. Two beads fell without issue but one got stuck. Regardless of how hard I blew, I couldn't get the bead to move.

The bell rang. Oh no! What am I to do? I sat quietly in my seat with one green bead lodged in my nose, pretending as if nothing had happened. Over the next hour, my face turned green. Panic-stricken, my teacher stared at me, asking if I was okay because she had no clue as to why my face was green. Scared to get in trouble, I didn't dare divulge what I had done.

Next thing I knew, I was in the emergency room with my mother. Now back then, one thing to never do was have your mom or dad miss time from work because of something you did. I knew I was in trouble. Honestly, I was more concerned about facing my mom than the procedure to remove the bead.

When I got home, she asked why I had done something so careless. I told the truth. I wanted to win the challenge. My mom gave me advice that I treasure to this day. "Never compete with anyone. If you do, you have already lost. In life, you should only compete with yourself. Compete to do your best."

Reflection Questions:
1. Which areas of your life are you fiercely and intentionally driven to win?
2. How are you competing? Who are you competing against?
3. How do you know if you are winning?

MY LIFE IS THE CHURCH

"Never feel guilty for doing what you love." - Ann

As a small child, the church was both the place I loved and resented, all at the same time. On most days, it was fun. However, there were times it interrupted things I wanted to do. Things like spending time with my friends or playing outside. My mom made me attend often and it felt as though we had a second address at the church. We went at least three times a week, Tuesday night Bible study, Thursday night choir rehearsal, sometimes on Saturday, and all day on Sunday. Sundays included Sunday School at 9:30 a.m., 11 a.m. worship service, and 6:30 p.m. night service.

In our house, church came first before everything else. I couldn't even fake an illness to stay at home. My mom would say, "If you're sick, okay. Church is the place for sick people."

The neighborhood children would tease my siblings and me about being "church children." To make matters worse, my dad bought my mom a 1962 black Ford Fairlane Station Wagon with a red interior to transport me, my siblings, aunt, and her children to church. The car would be packed and loaded down almost scrubbing the street. I would be so angry at my mom for making us go to church during the week when I'd rather be home watching television, talking on the telephone, or playing with my friends.

Once I got over the anger of having to go to church, I enjoyed the experience. Our church was very small, charismatic, and sanctified. We would attentively watch and listen to the "saints" sing, testify, dance, and shout. Let me tell you, some of the best original dances and dancers I've ever seen have been at church. In fact, I think some of those dances on television emanated from the church, such as The Jerk, The Slide, The Running Man, The Two-step, the James Brown, and some I can't even name.

At home, my siblings, cousins, and I would get a tambourine and mimic everything and everybody we saw at church and have what we called "play church." One day when playing church at my aunt's home, we made so much noise, the neighbor called the police, because it sounded like people were inside the house fighting. We were all scolded and threatened to within an inch of our lives never to do that again and instructed that God is not something or someone with whom we should play or making fun.

Because our church was small, my mother saw to it that her children got involved. Have you ever learned to play an instrument, because the church needed a player? Well, that is what happened to me. I learned how to play the piano because of the church. And early on, I played everything in the same key until I learned how to play better. I know I sounded horrible, but everyone encouraged me like I was Liberace. My brothers beat (mind you, I didn't say play) the drums, and my sister reluctantly directed the choir. In hindsight, we were church children, because this is all we knew and was ever exposed to.

Did I mention my uncle was the pastor and my other uncle (his brother) was the assistant pastor? My grandmother was the church mother, my mom was the Sunday School teacher, and all my mother's sisters and brothers were members. Each time I went to church, was like going to a large family reunion.

Our summer vacations would be wherever the annual church conference was being held, which was always something I looked forward to attending. Here, we got to meet people from across the country and develop lasting friendships and some marriages. We visited and toured places such as Washington D.C., Virginia Beach, Toronto, Tallahassee, Atlanta, and Cleveland, to name a few.

As I reflect on my life now that I am in my sixties, I did not stray from what was taught and instilled in me as a child. The church is and always has been an integral part of my life, and the "church comes first" commitment was easy until I became a wife and a mother. This commitment came with many sacrifices. There were many PTA meetings, school plays, outings, and activities I missed with my children because the church required my time.

At one point, I felt I was neglecting my children by being an absentee mother and not being more involved in what they were doing. My husband attended the PTA meetings so often most of the other mothers thought he was a single parent since they never saw me, and I rarely visited. I'm thankful my husband was understanding, willing and available to fulfill many obligations for me. Because of my commitment to the church, my husband knew who he was marrying, and he told me he would never stand between the church and me, nor would he ever ask me to choose.

The church is my spiritual walk, and it is my life. It's what and how I live each day, and it is first, whether I'm home, at the grocery store, shopping, out in the community, or inside the building we call CHURCH.

Now I cherish and fully understand who I am. I am the third-generation fruit of Charity's prayer "that God would bring forth fruit fit for His kingdom." MY LIFE IS THE CHURCH!!

Reflection Questions:
1. Have you ever felt guilty for doing something you love? Why or why not?
2. Which childhood activity shaped your life? Why?
3. Which experience have you had a love/hate relationship?

CHAPTER 7

JOY IN HEALTH

I JUST HAD A BABY, AND I STILL LOOK PREGNANT

"Look in the mirror, if you don't like what you see, make the changes needed."– Joy

I always thought being pregnant was the most wonderful feeling in the world. I looked forward to the days in which I could eat whatever I wanted with no regrets. It was my dream to marry my soulmate, wake him up at ridiculous hours of the night, and send him for the perfect food to satisfy my cravings.

Well, let's just say that during my first pregnancy, I really enjoyed eating guilt free. My favorite craving was ridged potato chips with sour cream and onion dip. Second to that was pizza with ranch dressing as the dipping sauce. Sounds horrible, right? No, it was really good!

I was excited to show early and wanted a perfectly round stomach to protrude as soon as possible. I was one happy mom to be. In fact, the more I "showed," the more I felt like a mom.

I was not concerned about my weight or counting calories, because I was eating for two. I gained thirty-four pounds while pregnant and delivered my baby at thirty-two weeks. Well, after having my beautiful bundle of joy, I still had fifteen pounds to go.

It was Christmas, and my baby was three weeks old. Prior to pregnancy, I was a size four. Now, I was wearing a size twelve and I was depressed. My husband went out and bought me a size twelve skirt and large top. I cried! Why was the weight not going away? Who wants to wear maternity clothes when you are not pregnant? Not me.

To make matters even worse, my sister-in-law, who had a baby one day before me, showed up on Christmas wearing her pre-pregnancy jeans. I was devastated. I asked my mom how I could lose the baby weight. She replied, "This is not baby weight; this is YOUR weight." Embedded in that experience and her comment was an invaluable lesson. Never lose focus of a long-term goal due to a short-term indulgence. To be successful, you must focus on both. I took my weight into my hands and created an action plan and I lost the pounds. Ladies, if you are not happy with your weight, stop making excuses and put a plan into action.

Reflection Questions:

1. Do you struggle with your weight? What excuses are you making (baby weight, middle-age spread, menopause, too many hours at work, etc.)?

2. What are you indulging in that creates a short-term pleasure to only be disappointed later?

3. Which new habits do you need to create to live a healthier life?

I HAVE A FEVER

"Ask questions about your family's health history." – Ann

What is wrong with me? I'm burning up inside with fever! Oh God, I'm so sick. I've never felt like this before. This must be really serious!

-Fast forward to two days later-

I'm sitting in my OB/GYN's office rattling off all kinds of nonsensical, random symptoms that I am having. I also start crying for no apparent reason—and I am not a crier. The doctor slightly shifts her head to the right, in deep thought, and looks at me with a strange stare and calmly says, "Sit here Mrs. Phillips, and I'll be right back."

I begin to have a serious internal conversation. *Just as I thought, it IS serious. She left the room to figure out how to break the terrible news to me.* Now I'm hyperventilating because my fears have taken over.

When she returns, laughing, she says, "Mrs. Phillips you're having hot flashes and I think you're premenopausal. I'm prescribing you some pills. In fact," she says while handing me some pills, "I strongly suggest you take one now."

At the age of forty-five, I thought I was too young to experience hot flashes, or even be premenopausal. I was advised by my doctor to ask my mother how old she was when it started happening to her, because it's very common for a daughter to follow the same menopausal path as her mother. Women, get to know your body. Don't be afraid to ask women in your family and please seek medical advice.

Reflection Questions:
1. What do you know about your family's health history?
2. Have you ever experienced a health scare? If so, what made you afraid?
3. Ask a woman (with whom you are close) to share weird symptoms in her body/health that she has experienced during various stages.

100TH BIRTHDAY CELEBRATION, PILLAR OF STRENGTH

"Charity Maples is my definition of strength."- Joy

It's June 4, 2018, the day my family has been waiting on for over a year. My great-grandmother turns 100 years of age. This is a special occasion as Charity Louisiana Maples, the matriarch of our family, is celebrating a century of life.

The last few weeks have been extremely hard as my great-grandmother has been in and out of the hospital experiencing what we've just learned is congestive heart failure. Day by day, it appears her heart is getting weaker and weaker. Likewise, she is becoming more fragile and less able to do things that were once, normal everyday activities.

Exactly one week ago, I got quite a scare. I was on vacation in Indianapolis and trying to sleep a little longer than normal. I awoke to my cell phone ringing. Startled, I looked at the phone and saw that it was my great-aunt Lois, who is the caretaker of my great-grandmother, calling from Memphis. I immediately got nervous, answered the phone, and said, "Lois, don't tell me anything bad. Is great-grandmother okay?" She replied, "Not really. We are in the hospital and she wants to talk to you."

"Little Joy is this you? Can you hear me? I'm calling to tell you that I love you. I really want you to know how much I love you. Your name is Joy and you are a fruit from the tree of the spirit. Your name means something. Do you hear me? You are a fruit from my tree, one of my generations. I want you to know that you are a STRONG woman. You are going to live a good life. I want you to live your name, Joy. When I get down and feeling bad, I think of Joy. The Joy of the Lord is my strength. You are my strength and my Joy. I was calling to tell you goodbye and that I love you," said my great-grandmother.

During the call, I began crying uncontrollably and could barely collect myself. I was a mess! All I could say was, "I love you too!" While I know that at some point in life, I will cherish her call, at the time, it felt like too much to bear.

For the next several days, my great-grandmother remained in the hospital. Every day, I prayed that God would allow her to live to see her 100th birthday. Not only did I want her to be alive, but I also wanted her to be alert and able to enjoy it. While in the hospital, she was singing, praying, and praising God. She talked so much that at times, my family would request that the doctors give her something to calm her down so she could rest. They never did, and she never stopped talking, dancing (praising God) in the bed, and singing.

She kept saying that she could feel music all through her body.

The day before her birthday, we got great news. Great-grandma got released from the hospital. On June 4th, the actual day of her birthday, I traveled with my daughter and sister to commemorate the momentous occasion at her home. We pulled up to the house, wearing our custom t-shirts with her photo on the front. I got out of the car with my camera and headed to the door to celebrate and take photos.

My great-aunt ran past the door, looked at me, and kept going. This was odd and strange. By the time I placed my hand on the doorknob, my aunt Lois frantically opened the door yelling, "She's gone. She's gone!" I think my heart almost stopped. I had a decision to make in a split second. Do I turn around and just break down, or do I walk in and try to deal with the image of seeing my great-grandmother transition into death?

Now let me be clear, I am the proverbial, "weeping Wanda," meaning that I am the last person you want witnessing something like that. More importantly, my aunt Lois is the most dramatic and unstable person I know in traumatic situations. Let me put it like this. If you are looking for the worst and most dramatic griever in life, you will find that individual in my aunt Lois.

I walked into the room to confront the situation.

"Oh my God. Momma wake up. Wake up," said Lois. "Oh, Lord. Oh, Jesus. Get her on the floor. Hurry up. The paramedics said to get her on the floor. Oh, Jesus. MOMMA!"

"Lois calm down. You are going to have to calm down." I grabbed her in a bear hug and tried to sit her down on the couch. "You are going to pass out," I said

I looked at my great-grandmother. She was sitting in her chair with her head slightly hanging down, and she appeared lifeless. Standing next to her was my grandmother, Ruth, who was very calm and composed as she gently rubbed her chest and spoke in her ear trying to wake her.

On the other side was a frail looking older man who I had never met. I thought to myself, *why is he trying to hand my dying great-grandmother a bouquet of yellow roses while we are attempting to restore her heart rate? Is that not the craziest thing?*

I looked back for my sister, Kristy, as I needed help and realized that she never made it into the house. I guess she chose option A and decided to have her own private meltdown in the driveway.

I jumped in front of my great-grandmother and began to try to lift her to put her on the floor.

"STOP! Be careful Joy. She's fragile. Make sure you don't hurt her. Oh, God. Oh, God." Pacing frantically and slipping on the sheet she was trying to put on the floor, my aunt Lois was in full panic and breakdown mode.

I stepped back and saw my great-grandmother raise her head. I immediately began to call her name trying to see if she could hear us. She looked up with the biggest and prettiest smile as if nothing had happened and said, "Joy, is that you? I see you."

Off in the distance, I heard this faint voice ask, "Ma'am are you there? Is the patient conscious?" It was the 911 operator who obviously had been on the phone listening and trying to get someone back on the line. In my aunt's panic, she had called the paramedics and then abandoned the phone.

Now I must admit in full disclosure, we were all a mess. However, the calmest person in the room was my great- grandmother. She was our strength. She looked up at me and said, "Get your phone and record me!" With tears in our eyes, we began to sing, "Happy Birthday." Fortunately, my dramatic sister Kristy had joined us in the house by that point.

I turned on the video capability on my cell phone and recorded her as she told a story about her life and her childhood. She spoke eloquently and was fully composed. You would have thought she was being interviewed by CNN. At one point, I had the audacity to look away while recording, and she said, "Joy, now you look at me and pay attention to me." And then she proceeded to finish recording the song she'd just made up on the spot.

"The Lord has blessed me to see my 100th birthday. The sun is shining for me each day. I found the answer when I learned to pray. He's been so good to me. He brought me from a long way. Yes, he has. He kept me down through the years. He is so good to me. Yes. He let me stay here so I could see y'all one more time. I don't know

how long I will be here with you, but I want you to know that I
praised the Lord for all of my days."

The paramedics arrived, and she sang gospel songs and offered compliments and encouragement to the paramedics as they completed their assessment of her. It was as if angels were in the room. *Now this is STRENGTH.* What an amazing woman. They were amazed and so were we. They wanted to rush her to the hospital, but she said no. She wanted to spend her birthday at home with family. They supported her decision and wished her a happy birthday.

God allowed my grandmother to have an amazing day. She was able to get dressed and take professional photos, enjoy company all day, and cut/eat her birthday cake. I know divine intervention allowed this. No one would have ever thought that we almost lost her hours prior.

I include this story because I believe her 100th birthday epitomizes the essence and strength of who she has been her entire life. She is one of the strongest women I have ever known. She is faithful, loving, funny, kind, beautiful, prophetic, honest, God-fearing, family-oriented, but most of all, my great-grandmother. While she tells me that my name means strength, she is the definition of STRENGTH!

"Now also when I am old and gray-headed, O God, forsake me not; until I have shewed thy strength unto this generation, and thy power to everyone this is to come." (Psalm 71:18 KJV)

Reflection Questions:
1. Who is the pillar of strength in your family?
2. Describe a time in your life in which you had to rely on a higher level of strength? What were the things or people that gave you hope?
3. What is the legacy you want to leave and why?

A HARD LABOR

"When you are afraid, you will find peace in prayer. God answers prayers."-Charity

I was terrified to have a baby. My mother died in childbirth and I was afraid I was going to suffer a similar fate. Daily, I prayed that God would let me survive the birth of my first child. I was both excited and petrified. I shielded my internal turmoil from the outside world by hiding behind a fake smile. No one knew how I honestly felt.

In the 1920s, because Black women did not go to the hospital to have babies and instead had them at home, many mothers and children died during delivery. I remember the day the pains started. At first, it felt like a sharp cramp, similar to what a woman might experience when she's menstruating. Then the awkward cramps evolved into pain. Unrelenting pain that moved from my stomach to my back. It felt like something was balling up into a knot in my stomach, making it hard and unbearable, and then slightly subside only to start over again. I tried to hide what was happening and the accompanying pain because I feared it might be my last day on earth.

When my husband came home from work, he immediately recognized that I was in excruciating pain. He got a woman—maybe a midwife—to help. When she arrived, I became excited as I assumed she had a solution to help ease the pain. WRONG. She came in and grabbed some black pepper and added it to a pot of water. She made the water as hot as I could bear. She then told me to drink the hot pepper water mixture. It burned! I was already hurting and that made it terrible. I got angry. She was supposed to help but she only made things worse. I couldn't believe pain could be so raw, real, and severe. The woman said the pepper was meant to make the contractions harder, so I could push the baby out. In today's world, this would be called an herbal way to induce labor. Upset, I said to my husband, "That woman can't do nothing for me." It was inevitable; I was not going to make it through the delivery. I prayed even harder.

My father came over as he heard the news that I wasn't doing well during the labor. He walked into the room, looked me in the eyes, and said, "Chat Lou, I'm going to help you." He washed his hands, rolled up his sleeves, and greased his arms. He came back in the room and said, "Chat Lou, don't be ashamed, I got to do what I got to do." I closed my eyes. I wasn't ashamed as I was in horrible pain and I wanted relief. Papa grabbed this baby out of me. He delivered her. She came out feet first. He got her out, thank God.

Then, the midwife took over and cut the navel string. I was hurting from one end to the next. I knew something was torn as babies weren't supposed to come out feet first. I also knew without my dad, I would not have survived childbirth. I also didn't have any medicine to ease the pain. I laid in bed for nine days, trying to heal and recover from that dreadful experience.

I was thankful and grateful as I had given birth to a healthy, beautiful baby girl. Deep down in my heart, I always wanted a girl. Now it was time to name her. My husband's mother name was Rena, and my husband's middle name was Joe Austin. Jorethus was the name he liked but I didn't care for it. So, we named her Jorene after both—Jo from his middle name and Rena from his mom. Thank God for sparing my life and blessing me with a beautiful daughter.

Reflection Questions:
1. In what situation have you had to face fear?
2. What surprised you in this story?
3. What is one thing you can do differently when faced with fear?

THE "C" WORD

"Know your body, examine your body, and listen to your body."- Taylor

There are moments in life when you feel as though everything is about to fall apart. This was one of those days.

Two years ago, I was living my best life. Everything was going as planned: college, my own apartment, friends, and school. (Yep, I separated college from school but that is an entirely different matter.) A few months prior, I started birth control but it was something I took cautiously. My mother had given me advice and I listened to everything she said with a grain of salt.

When your doctor prescribes birth control, they tell you a few important things. One is to do a monthly self-breast exam which, to me, was always strange. It felt like checking fruit for bruises. Except, what was I supposed to do if the fruit wasn't good? I only have two breasts and I can't put them back if they're bad. Therefore, I did the breast exam religiously.

One day, I was staring at my reflection in the mirror and felt a lump. I felt it before I touched it. For a few weeks, I had been having a sharp pain in the right side of my right breast. I brushed it off and attributed it to discomfort that comes with my menstrual cycle. It wasn't until I felt it with my hands that I got scared. I couldn't bring myself to call it a lump. Therefore, I took my phone and immediately called my family doctor, aka my mother. As usual, she told me not to worry and that she would book a doctor's appointment for me. She scheduled the appointment for the following day.

Little did she know, that put fear into my heart. My mother never booked anything with any type of urgency. Procrastination was her middle name. Now, I was nervous. It wasn't until I went to the doctor that I became terrified. I was a few months' shy of taking birth control for a year and it was time to figure out what was going on.

The next morning, an overwhelming smell of hand sanitizer and bleach filled my nostrils as I sat waiting for the doctor to see me. "You can put on this robe and have a seat up here. The doctor will be with you shortly." I went from feeling like a piece of fruit in my room to feeling like a piece of meat being tested for salmonella. I laid still on the table with the paper gown uncomfortably wrapped around me as the openness of my back pressed against the white paper used to eliminate the presence of the person that had been there before me. *Why were they here?* Was it something simple like a cold or were they there like me, fearing more? In my solitude, I prayed for the stranger that was only minutes before, in my position. That gave me comfort.

Knock. Knock. My doctor entered the room and for the first time, I remembered my mother was there with me because it was the first time she spoke. Again, that is rare. The doctor asked me a few questions and before I knew it, the chill of her hand was upon me. Although the doctor said a lot, the only phrases I heard were, "I am concerned," and "I want to schedule you for a mammogram."

Let's be clear, there's not a twenty-year-old in the world who wants to hear those words. Didn't I have several more years before needing to worry about a mammogram? Wasn't I safe from this type of thing? I lived in a bubble and guess what? In that moment, it popped.

For the first time in my life, I experienced real fear. There's fear of roller coasters when your stomach drops or fear of spiders and crawly things. Then there is the fear of death. I had never been confronted with the fact that I could be so sick that I could die. Therefore, I did what most frightened people do, I avoided my problem. For weeks, I let the nurse's calls about booking my appointment go to voicemail. One month soon passed and I received a call from my actual doctor. This was when I paid attention. She informed me that since I was not proactive, she would book the appointment for me. I didn't even know that doctors did that. NOW, I was beyond terrified. In my mind, this meant she thought I had the C word. It's still hard for me to even spell it out.

Finally, I called back and explained that we had an upcoming family vacation. All I asked was to have the appointment scheduled for after the trip. I did not want to be on vacation facing new realities depending on how my appointment went.

Once I returned from vacation, it was time to face reality. Every night, I put my hands over that area of tissue and prayed over it. My doctor had taken me off birth control to see if there were any changes. Unfortunately, there were none. I began to sweat the small stuff. Will it hurt? Do I even have enough breast tissue to squeeze between two metal plates? Will they have to take my breasts? Will I go bald? Your mind is truly sometimes your greatest enemy. I had diagnosed myself and hadn't even had the appointment yet.

Eventually, it was appointment day and my mother was right by my side. She never said it, but I saw the fear in her eyes. Her silence spoke louder than any words. They called my name and it was my turn. Luckily, because of my age, they decided to do an ultrasound instead of a mammogram. That helped ease some of my internal worry. Next, I undressed and followed the nurse into a dark room. I thought, *why in the world do they have the lights out?* Subconsciously, I always equated light with the presence of God and darkness to the devil. I had to push that to the back of my mind as the chill of the cold gel on my breast snapped me back to reality.

My eyes searched the black and white monitor as they took pictures and examined what was happening inside of my body. I don't think my heart had ever beat so fast.

While I was getting checked for one thing, I feared being admitted due to an anxiety attack. The woman explained that the results would take a few days but based on what she could see, I had a cyst and not the other C word. Finally, I could breathe. I literally tasted the salt in my tears of relief from the news. I was informed that I had dense breast tissue and fibrocystic breasts. When they let me off that table, my mom and I hugged and started shouting (praising God in a dance). I didn't care that I was half naked in an office, I was just thankful. The fear and anxiety I had been dealing with was over. They told me that I might have to get the cyst removed and that my breast would probably never stand at attention, but I didn't give a flying flip. My prayers were answered and I was reminded of a few valuable lessons.

First, my mother had given me sage advice. Second, it is important to know your body, examine your body, and listen to your body. Finally, prayer works. Just as I prayed for someone I didn't know; I found peace in feeling like someone had also done it for me.

Reflection Questions:
1. What were your thoughts when reading this story?
2. What fears do you have regarding your health?
3. How often do you pray and how does it impact you?

BREASTFEEDING WAS NOT FOR ME

"Every woman needs a good girdle. It teaches your body how to stay tight." - Joy

B reastfeeding has been said to be the best and most natural way to feed your baby. Unfortunately, I didn't nurse my first child but I wanted to try it with my second. I did the research and even took a class on this new experience. I was thrilled to learn the benefits for both baby and mother. Having friends tell me that nursing helped them quickly lose baby weight sealed the deal. How could I pass up this wonderful opportunity for my baby? And I could lose a couple of extra pounds. Sign me up!

I bought all the necessary equipment to prepare, including nursing bras and a breast pump to express milk. Because I would return to work in a couple of months, I wanted an option for the baby to bond with my husband during night feedings and offer a solution for my caretaker. I was excited.

On June 18, 1999, I gave birth to my beautiful son, Tyron Phillip Fitzgerald Jr. Hours after the delivery, the nurse brought the baby into the room and said, "Mom are you ready to nurse?" I was a little nervous as I'd heard it might hurt. I had undergone thirty-six hours of labor and was not up for any more pain. I wasn't worried about milk production, as I had gone from a bra size 32 C to a 36 G! I would have milk for months. I looked at the nurse and said, "Yes."

I held my little blessing close and began to see if he would latch on to my breast. I was thinking, "Please let this baby attach and this not hurt." He successfully attached. I was excited. I thought, *this is not so bad. I can do this*. It felt a little funny and hurt just a tad bit, but overall it was not painful or a bad experience.

Just as I was getting comfortable with nursing, my husband turned and said, "Joy, are you doing that right? I think your breast is going to smother him. It looks like his nose is too close to your breast. Should we call the nurse?" Okay, I began to worry if I was doing it right. I didn't want to smother my baby.

"Babe, call the nurse." The nurse came in and said that everything was okay but to make sure that I didn't fall asleep nursing the baby because in rare cases, a mom could smother the baby if she puts an unreasonable amount of pressure over the baby's nose. Keep in mind, this is for women with large breasts.

I was released from the hospital. Later that evening, I tried the breast pump. I went into the nursery, got relaxed, and started the machine. The machine consisted of two long tubes that connected to a box. At the end of each long tube, there was a suction cup that attached to the nipple. I placed the suction cups on my breasts and hit the power button. The machine was loud and sounded awful. Sitting there, I began to cry. Nothing about what I was doing felt natural or comfortable. I felt fat, tired, overwhelmed, and now, like a cow. Plus, the machine took forever!

I hated pumping but I didn't want to tell anyone. If I expressed my true feelings, I might seem ungrateful or pretentious. So, I decided to wipe my tears and grab the two bags of milk and head back into the room with my family and pretend that everything was okay. I sat on the couch and tried to figure out why I wanted to cry. *Get it together Joy; it's your hormones. Pull yourself together. You will be okay. This will get better.*

My son adapted to nursing quite well. However, he wanted to nurse all the time. I couldn't tell if he was hungry or if he just liked nursing. At least with a bottle, I could tell how much milk he was getting. With nursing, I never knew. I felt like I was always feeding him, 24/7. I persevered and kept nursing because it was best for him but I seriously disliked it.

One day, I was home and my mom stopped by to check on the baby. I was wearing one of my husband's t-shirts and a pair of jogging pants. Now for the record, my husband wears a large and before the pregnancy, I wore an extra small. Now, I could reasonably fit his large shirt.

When I opened the door, my mom smiled and asked, "Hey, where is the baby?" She looked at me funny.

"Mom, what is so funny?"

"Well, your breasts and back have gotten so big. Girl, you look like a linebacker."

"Thanks, Mom."

"Well, I'm not trying to hurt your feelings. But I am your mom and I'm just telling you the truth. Are your breasts going to get any bigger?"

"I don't know, but truth be told, I hate this!"

"Well, why are you doing it?"

"Everyone says that it's best for the baby but I'm tired, exhausted, and nursing all the time. I am ready to quit. I have to go back to work in two weeks and he's still not adjusting to the bottle."

"Well, I think you should do what works best for YOU! Quit feeling guilty. This is your body."

"Thanks. I needed to hear that. I'm quitting today! I feel fat. I have to eat all day. I'm tired. This is just not for me. Plus, I have Taylor who needs attention as she is feeling a little neglected since the baby has gotten here, and I am going back to work still looking pregnant. I have NO time because I'm nursing all the time."

I had been waiting for someone to tell me that it was alright to quit. I immediately got on the phone and called the nursing consultant to discuss the best way to wean the baby off my breast and onto a bottle. It didn't work. I was continuing to produce milk every two hours. So, I decided that I would quit cold turkey. Big mistake.

My breast became extremely swollen and were hurting badly. I called the nurse back and she told me to take some pain medication and wait it out. Again, it was not working. I never thought my breasts could hurt so much. They were inflamed and had a fever in them.

I knew what to do. I called my great-grandmother. "Grandma, I am trying to dry up my milk. What should I do? They are huge and hurting."

"Baby, do you have a cabbage in the house?"

"No, what is the cabbage for?"

"Well, cabbage will draw out the fever and inflammation in your breasts and help to dry them up. The leaves in the cabbage are full of water. Take a cabbage and peel the big leaves from the outer part and stick them into a tight bra all around your breasts. You will begin to see that the leaves will dry out as your breasts will absorb all the moisture and water. When the leaves become dry, remove them, and replace with new ones. Keep doing that until the leaves stay moist. Then you'll know that the inflammation is gone and your milk is drying out."

"Grandma, I have never heard of this. Are you sure it will work?"

"Yes, call me back and let me know how it is going. Oh, and don't forget to wear a girdle every day to pull your stomach in. This will train your body and keep you tight. Don't teach your body to hang, teach it to tighten up. I had eight babies and I never had a problem with weight. Do what I tell you now, you hear?"

Now I know this sounds crazy, but I did it. I walked around the house for two days with cabbage hanging out of my bra. But guess what, it worked. They stopped hurting, the swelling went down, and there was no longer fever in my breasts. Also, the milk stopped producing! Yes, thank God for great-grandparents.

Now ladies, I share this story not to discourage any woman from nursing, as I fundamentally believe this is the best option for both the baby and the mother. However, I want women to know that breastfeeding is not the only option. I want to encourage you to make the best decision for you, your baby, and your lifestyle. Nursing isn't for everyone and that is totally fine. Don't beat yourself up about it. It's a personal choice. Feel good about your decision.

Women, it's alright to acknowledge the many feelings and insecurities we face during and after pregnancy. We go through so many emotions and rarely share how we feel. Express your feelings. Find a friend, mother, or another woman who will allow you to be vulnerable and acknowledge your emotions. This is healthy and necessary as healing takes place both internally and externally. We rarely recognize the internal healing that is needed.

I know many of you will read this story and get angry at my mom for what she said—don't! My mother knew me best and knew that I was miserable. She needed to find a funny way to tell me what I needed to hear. This is our relationship and I love it. Oh, and for those who are nursing or may nurse, know that cabbage can be your best friend!

Reflection Questions:

1. Which friend could you offer support for during and after pregnancy?

2. After reading this story, what have you experienced in your body that you struggle with but refuse to acknowledge? (this doesn't have to be about pregnancy)

3. How can you better support the internal healing that women need as they experience different stages in life?

CHAPTER 8

SAGE ADVICE AND WISDOM

This is a compilation of life lessons, advice, words of wisdom, and home remedies that have been passed on and shared with me from some very wise women, in addition to some of my own personal experiences. I treasure this knowledge, because it has helped me along my journey of becoming a healthy and happy mother, wife, and successful woman!

"The only thing to do with good advice is to pass it on. It is never of any use to oneself."
—*Oscar Wilde*

PEARLS OF KNOWLEDGE
Taylor

TAKE ADVANTAGE OF YOUR EDUCATION

College was an absolute blast. You leave with an education, but if you didn't take anything away from that education, you did not take full advantage. Study abroad, join clubs, meet new people, discover different types of foods and restaurants, become a local somewhere, or go and sit and talk to your professors. The possibilities that the right college offers are endless. Freshman year, I did not take advantage of these experiences. Instead, I kept my head in the books. It wasn't until my sophomore year that I realized I had missed out on so much. When you leave college, all you are left with are memories and knowledge. If you leave with only knowledge and no memories or worthwhile experiences, you have missed out!

KEEP IT CLEAN...I SMELL YOU!

I cannot tell you how many times I have been out in public and nauseated by the smell of a female's body odor. As women, we all know that smell. When you are on your cycle, it can literally smell like dead fish if you are not taking the right measures. Ladies, think of your vagina like a flower. Flowers need to be watered, trimmed, exposed to sunlight, and they need to be in a clean environment. When someone gives you flowers, the first thing you do is find a vase to put them in. No one ever goes and grabs a dirty vase. Your flower is the same way. Keeping a clean environment is essential.

A common misconception is soap. Your flower maintains its pH balance naturally, and some soaps do more harm than good causing yeast infections. Flowers also need to have their stems cut. Similarly, it's important to trim your flower as hair can trap bad odors and smells. However, if you cut off the entire stem, the flower would die. Hair can also protect certain areas from harmful bacteria, so a little never hurt anybody. Next, you need to add some water to the vase but take note not to add hot water. Your flower is the same. Hot water can throw off your pH balance as well. Finally, the flower needs exposure to the sun and the opportunity to take in CO_2. Your flower is no different. Wearing underwear 24/7, especially tight non-cotton underwear, prevents your flower from breathing. Bacteria thrives in hot, sticky places. Try sleeping without underwear sometimes and letting your flower breathe. If that is too uncomfortable, wear loose shorts at bedtime.

Flowers are meant to smell good and give off a fresh aroma. If a flower is not taken care of properly, it will die and leave a bad odor. Please take care of your flower. I do not want to smell you.

Note: This is my personal advice and not meant to replace medical expertise.

SAYING GOODBYE IS NOT ALWAYS A BAD THING

This will be quick. Not every friend will be a lifelong friend and that is not a bad thing. Knowing when to say goodbye to someone in an amicable way is a lesson that will take you far. Everyone is not meant to be on your bus or in your life. The more weight on the bus, the more gas you will need to push it forward. So, don't be afraid to say goodbye to the people that create more burden than benefit in your life.

IT'S YOUR LIFE

Parents are great. They are sometimes our heroes. However, as we grow up, we are faced with the reality that they are not perfect and do not have all the answers. I used to do whatever made my parents happy. But this is my life to live, not theirs. Additionally, with age comes responsibility. The adult decisions that I make will have a lasting impact on me, not my parents. That is why it is vital to make decisions that will make you happy in the long run.

Regretting a decision that you have made feels different from regretting a decision that was made *for* you. This advice is not just regarding parents, but rather anyone, friends, boyfriends, church members, family members, etc. Don't let life happen to you. Make life happen. Choosing the college I wanted to attend was the first decision I made for myself and I had the time of my life. I am living my best life and I encourage you to do the same.

CLUTCHING MY PEARLS
Joy

MARRY YOUR BEST FRIEND

Marriage is one of the best decisions I've ever made. As it relates to what one should look for in marriage, the advice is endless. There are many books and stories available and even marriage counselors to help people understand the secret sauce of marriage. For me, the answer was simple; marry your best friend. My best advice to anyone considering marriage, please marry your friend, not the person that you are infatuated with because that will come and go in a relationship. Marry a person with whom you enjoy spending time. When you've left your family and friends to live in a city that only has two seasons (winter & fall), and it's just the two of you in the house for a long winter, you will need a friend and a spouse bundled into one.

Another thing, you should enjoy spending time with the person more than anyone else. We struck gold in this area! My husband and I started out as friends and that foundation has been the key to keeping us together for over twenty-four years. We do EVERYTHING together and we love it. He is the first person that I want to tell my best and worst news. He is my favorite hello and saddest goodbye. Tyron is my Best Friend for Life and I am lucky to be his WIFE.

A SACRIFICE MADE

One of the most significant challenges I faced in life was relocating to Cedar Rapids, Iowa. I didn't want to move to the Midwest, nor did I want to be someplace cold that lacked diversity in representation of people that looked like me. I loved Memphis. I was born and raised there and it was home for all of my family. I had two children and my mother and grandmother had been my supporters and reliable help. How could I leave my parents, sisters, niece, and nephew? I loved my church, book club, and my established network of friends. However, my husband had a great job opportunity and wanted to move.

Throughout our entire marriage, he was selfless. He always put the children and me first. This was the one time that I knew he wanted to do something that I was against. How could I say no to a man who always said yes to me? I couldn't. So, I packed up my family and went to cold, minimal diversity, Cedar Rapids. I was devastated, depressed, and missed everything about home. Tyron asked me to trust him as he believed the move had something good in store for us. Well, he was right. I finished my Master's degree, met two new amazing friends that I now call family, and blossomed in my career! I learned that no great reward is without great sacrifice. I also learned to trust my husband and believe in him even when the path is not clear to me.

IT IS OKAY TO ASK FOR HELP

Being raised in the South, there are many rules for, and expectations of women. My mom taught me all of them, even the ones in which I didn't agree. In our home, there were certain things that women did and certain things that men did. Women raised the children, took responsibility for the household chores, cooked, and worked a full-time job. Men just worked and took care of the outside of the home to include lawn care, cars, etc. At one point in my career, I worked and traveled quite a bit. On Saturdays, I spent the entire day cleaning and washing. On Sundays, I spent the whole day at church. I was exhausted. I remember saying to my mom that I needed to hire a housekeeper. You would have thought I said a bad word. She looked at me and said that the home was my job. She then went on a rant about how she did everything and never had help and that it didn't kill her.

This is the one time that I am glad that I didn't take her advice. I hired a housekeeper and it was one of the best decisions I made because I was able to be more present with my family on the weekends and more delightful to my children as I was not always stressing over the house. Well, guess what? After a couple of months, my mom got a housekeeper as well. I guess the younger generation can teach the older generation a few things. Just know, we don't have to repeat everything our parents did. Keep the good and replace the old with new more efficient habits.

INTERNET DOCTOR

Stay off the internet for health advice. At one point in my life, I became addicted to the Internet for information and relied on it as my personal physician. I was a member of several health forums and would discuss my health with strangers. Needless to say, I diagnosed myself with multiple conditions and illnesses. Thankfully, I met a doctor who strongly encouraged me to STAY OFF THE INTERNET. Amazingly, after I got off the Internet for medical advice, I have lived my healthiest life. The Internet is the last place you should go and seek medical advice from random people. Instead, seek licensed professional advice regarding your health.

RAISING CHILDREN

My children are my greatest joy and I've enjoyed raising them. They are obedient and have been a pleasure to parent through the young stages of life. From an early age, one of the fundamental values I instilled was respect. I didn't allow my children to fall out on the floor, throw things, talk back, or hit me. Those were clear lines of disrespect in our home. When my children were little, if they misbehaved, I did not yell. Instead, I would get on my knees and meet them at eye level. Then, in a soft but stern voice, I would tell them that their behavior was unacceptable and to stop. They would. I managed my children through the tone of my voice and look on my face. They knew when I was serious and when I was playing. I was consistent and didn't settle for anything less than obedience. I didn't make excuses for bad behavior that I often hear from moms such as, "They're just sleepy." Seriously, they are not sleepy all the time. I addressed the behavior at a young age, and it has paid off. I advise all moms to teach your children to obey and respect authority. It might be the very thing that saves their life.

DON'T BE TOO STRICT

My parents had me when they were young. I know that they did the best they could and I think I turned out alright. However, they were very strict. In my opinion, too strict. I grew up in a Holiness Church that had tons of rules. Girls couldn't wear pants, make-up, or fingernail polish. Nor could we listen to R&B music, wear our toes out in shoes, have dye in our hair, and so many more things. Imagine having all of these rules as a young girl. It was overwhelming.

I loved the church, but I felt like I didn't have a childhood. I was denied so many experiences that when I went to college, I tried to experience everything that I couldn't while in my parent's home. Based on my experiences, I made a promise that if I ever had children, I would provide them balance and options in life. I would allow them to discover who they are and what they desired. They would lack this understanding if I never allowed them choices. While I am not an advocate of children having total freedom, as they need structure and parents, they should also enjoy being young and experiencing self-discovery.

Now, this advice is not to belittle or judge my childhood in the church but to acknowledge that we need to allow children to have healthy experiences. When I went to college, I didn't know who I was because everything in life had been defined for me. Thankfully, I made good decisions. But I saw many girls and boys who didn't because they didn't know how to deal with freedom and choices. Many young ladies in college had terrible relationships with their mom because they resented their childhood and lacked a healthy relationship. They made bad choices and some even got into trouble. While it wasn't my journey, it could have been. Thankfully, my mom gave me the space to grow as a young adult and had an open conversation with me about what she would have done differently given the chance. This conversation liberated me and made me love her even more!

PEARLS OF WISDOM AND SAGE ADVICE
Ann

WEIGHT

There's a true saying that time brings about a change. As a small child and well into my late thirties, I could eat anything and as much as I desired and never gain a pound of weight. In fact, I had maintained a consistent weight and wore the same size clothing and shoes throughout my adult life, which also included two pregnancies.

This was a huge benefit in allowing me to accumulate a vast wardrobe, because my size never changed. People would often remark, "You sure do have a lot of clothing." I would say, "This is old," due to the fact I never had to upsize my wardrobe, but only upgrade.

Then, every five-year span after the age of thirty brought about a change. Somehow weight seemed to just appear without warning. My eating habits had not changed so what was happening? I would go to bed at night and wake up three to five pounds heavier. Weight management had become an issue.

Don't let your weight become unmanageable before you react. The first thing I did was to assign myself a healthy weight range (that would allow me to fit inside all those clothes I had accumulated). I knew my maximum weight range number and began weighing myself every morning. If my weight started nearing that maximum number, I knew I had to be proactive in getting it back down by eating better and exercising. A three-to-five-pound weight loss management goal is much easier than twenty or thirty pounds.

PREGNANCY WEIGHT

Birthing a baby terrified me. I probably asked my mother if having a baby was as painful and difficult as some of the horror stories I'd heard. She told me that if I didn't gain too much weight (have a large baby) and only gained around twenty pounds, I'd have an easy delivery. She said the difficulty in labor centered around the baby's size in relation to the birth canal.

I did as my mom advised, only gaining twenty-one pounds. My labor was four hours, and I had a six-pound four-ounce baby. The upside is that I was able to wear all my clothes without having to lose any baby fat. A word to the wise, "Eat like you're carrying a baby, and not like you're carrying a cow."

When I came home from the hospital, my mother made me wear a panty girdle to hold my stomach and firm up the muscles so that I would not have a baby gut. Believe it or not, I am in my sixties, and my stomach is and always has been flat except when I was pregnant. I have never had a bulging stomach. Work on your body consistently and continuously, especially after the baby!

YOUR BODY

Take good care of your body while you're young, and it will pay off when you're older. I can't tell you how many times I've heard my grandmother say this to me. One thing she would remark about was not to ruin your kidneys, because we could not have hers.

My grandmother would not drink sodas or anything but clear liquids. Instead of drinking coffee, she would drink a cup of warm water every morning as it was the best way to purify and get your system moving. Think about it, when you go to the hospital, the first thing they give you is an IV...water.

BEAUTIFUL SKIN

My great aunt always had beautiful, soft skin. Her facial complexion was smooth and blemish free. Her secret was that she never put soap on her face. She only washed her face with warm water and then oiled it with olive oil. Our family (due to Native American heritage) have high cheekbones and darkening under the eyes. My sister told me to use aloe vera oil every day under my eyes to rid the darkening. It works. Try it if you're experiencing darkening under the eyes.

HOME REMEDY

One of the best home remedies for nausea and indigestion was given to me by my grandmother. She would take orange peels and let them dry and harden until she could break them into small little pieces, put them in a small, plastic bag, and store them in her purse. She would often have what she called sick spells. When she felt ill, she would put a chip of the peel under her tongue and suck on it until she felt better. This is a tried and true remedy that works.

SOMETHING TO PONDER - THE GLOVES

My great aunt (now deceased) owned several pairs of hand gloves, all different colors, and would only wear the gloves when she went out in public. One day, I asked her why she wore gloves. She told me that men were nasty and didn't wash their hands after using the restroom and would always want to shake her hand. The thought of them having just touched themselves, not washing their hands, and then wanting to touch her was repulsive. The gloves were a barrier to protect her from their dirty hands.

NO BAD DAYS

I was visiting my grandmother one day and she asked, "How is your day?" I replied that I was having a bad day. Oh, my God. Why did I say that? She began to chastise me, "God did not make bad days. The scripture said that everything God made was good. This is the day that the Lord has made. Let us rejoice and be glad in it. Don't you ever let that come out of your mouth again."

My grandmother believes that words have self-prophetic power and to be careful to always choose your words wisely before speaking. In hindsight, she wanted me to tell her what I had been doing that day. Since that time, I say that I have good days and better days, because I do not have bad days.

MEDICINE BLESSING

We've all been taught as small children to pray over and bless our food before we eat. But have you ever thought about blessing your medicine before taking it?

I once observed my grandmother praying over her medicine before she took it, and I told her that I had never thought about doing that. She said, "Praying over and blessing the medicine is more serious and important than the food, because we don't know what they're putting in the medicine. These people could be slowly poisoning us and we don't know it."

I laughed, but realized the value of this pearl of wisdom. I now pray over my medications that the Lord would bless them to serve the intended purpose and not to cause harm.

WHAT IS A BAD WORD?

I was babysitting my grandchildren one weekend and they were keeping up a lot of noise. So, I told them to "shut up and be quiet." My grandson said, "Ooo wee Nana, you said a bad word." I asked what I had said that was bad. He replied, "You said shut up. Mommy says that's a bad word."

I snickered and apologized and promised not to say it again. I asked my daughter why she told her children that. She said she didn't think it was nice to hear little children saying shut up. Instead, she would say "be quiet." I, on the other hand, taught my children that "hate" and "lie" were bad words.

My mother taught me never to use the word hate as it related to another person and especially about my sister or brothers. She also said that using the word "lie" was not appropriate for a child, and that only grown-ups could use that word. We were taught to say, "You told something that ain't so." Even now as an adult, I still don't use hate and rarely, if ever, use the word lie. This is evidence that your children are a product of whatever you teach them.

IT'S YOUR BABY

I told my daughters to be very sure they were ready for a baby before having one. I taught them not to expect anyone to take the responsibility of caring for the child, because ultimately, it would all fall on them as mothers. Sure, you would get help from time-to-time, but not to expect it and be grateful when you did.

HALF A CENTURY

Turning fifty was traumatic. I keep repeating to myself, "I'm half a century." I realized that I was probably at the pinnacle of my life and would probably not live another 50 years. Talk about scary and depressing...

My husband and daughters insisted on giving me a "surprise" landmark birthday party, which was the first birthday party I'd ever had. I don't like being fussed over or being the center of attention. I wandered around in my "50-year funk" for a few months. Seriously, I was traumatized.

I don't know when it happened, but one day I arose with a calmness, vision, and focus. I know it must've been the Lord, because I realized how blessed I was. There are so many people who did not and will not live to see fifty years. My vision was now to begin making new memories, doing new things, traveling to new places, meeting new people, and trying new hobbies.

I was in a new season of my life and I wanted to embrace and enjoy it to the fullest. It's now time to fulfill those bucket list items. I am focused on the things closest to my heart: my husband, my children, and most importantly, my grandchildren. I want to start creating good memories with them. I want them to have good, fun, and wholesome stories to pass on to their children about their grandmother as I do about my grandmother.

I began spending more time with them, taking them places I grew up, to the family cemeteries, showing them their deceased relatives and where they're buried. I have always taken them on an annual vacation. Now we venture to places outside the United States to expand their horizons.

I do fun and silly stuff with them too. I understand the value of being a grandmother and I want to be the best in their sight. I began sharing family stories and tales that were told to me when I was a child. I now find myself thinking of all the new experiences, fun things, and places I can take them. With clarity, vision, and focus, I am truly enjoying my new SEASON of life!

WISDOM
Ruth

WHAT HAPPENED TO YOUR WAIST?

For years, I've been saying that "low riding" jeans, pants, and skirts were the worst clothes ever made for women. Oh, and let's not leave out bikini panties. I know I'm old-fashioned in a lot of my views, but I like to tell it like it is. When I was a girl, women had defined waistlines and clothes were made as such with waistlines. It was a badge of honor to have a shape like a Coca-Cola bottle! But now, women have shapes like Coke cans and liter bottles. Why? Glad you asked. The aforementioned type of clothing has afforded women the privilege of not having to be concerned about their stomach sizes, because the low riding clothes fit under the stomach. I prescribe to wearing good undergarments (girdles or Spanx if necessary) to enhance a nice shape instead of letting it all hang out with a "done-lap" (that's when your belly done lapped over the top of your pants). I'm not as small as I once was, but I can assure you that I still have a waistline at eighty years of age.

YES, YOU DO KNOW

I'm known for being very inquisitive, some may even call me nosey. People don't tell me gossip because they know I'll ask too many questions, i.e., "Who told you that? Did you see this for yourself?" The response is usually, "I don't know." My theory is, if you can't tell me where you heard it or who told you, don't come to me with it. When my children would misbehave or get into trouble, and I'd ask what they'd done or what were they thinking, the prevailing answer was always, "I don't know." A response that often caused more problems for them, than telling me the truth. I taught my children to always answer me when I asked them a question. My response to the "I don't know" answer was, "Yes you do know and we're going to sit here until you tell me." Sometimes a response might've had a little coaxing with discipline, but I would not let them get away with, "I don't know."

SEX OR FIGHT

I in no way condone a man hitting a woman and for the sake of anonymity, I'll just say that I knew a married couple and they appeared happily married. Then suddenly, he started treating her mean and would sometimes fight her. Because I never saw that side of her husband, only him being loving and giving, I was confused. One day I asked her why he'd been mistreating her. She said, "Because I won't have sex with him because I'm angry, so he's on punishment." I was shocked by her response. I told her, "You know what, that's silly! You'd rather have him fight and be mean to you, than to sleep with your own husband? You're his wife and you need to sleep with him if you are going to stay with him."

If you are married, sex is an important part of the relationship. Have sex with your husband at least a couple of times a week. Why argue for hours over sex? That's crazy. You wasted three or four hours arguing over something that could have been over in five to ten minutes. Just think, you missed out on three hours of sleep for nothing!

SAGE ADVICE
Charity Maples

LOVE YOUR CHILDREN

"Children are precious in the eyesight of the Lord because only God can give life." My heart mourns for the children and what they must face in today's world. If we as "mothers" don't teach our children, we will have a lost generation. Mothers, love your children and keep them in prayer before the Lord. Teach them to obey and to respect you. Teach them how to pray, how to love, and how to forgive.

NO FIGHTING

I never allowed my children to fight each other. Instead, I taught them to love and respect their sisters and brothers. Oh, they had their share of spats and disagreements, but they knew better than to let me see them fighting. If, perchance, they did fight, I would immediately stop it and make them hug and say they were sorry. It was not always easy because children can sometimes be stubborn. I would persevere until they did what I told them to do. I believed that if I allowed them to fight as small children, and say ugly things to one another, this would grow up in them as adults.

"Adults are just outdated children." —Dr. Seuss

LET'S PLAY

Living in rural Mississippi (back then) was much different than it is now. We didn't have televisions and video games like the children do today. It was easy to have "family time" and to talk and play. I played games with my children. Some, we even made up and we had fun! I would tell them stories or tales that were told to me when I was a child. I purposed in my heart that my children would never feel alone because if they had nothing else, they had me. Mothers enjoy your children at all times.

"Your children should mean the world to you, but to them, you are the world."

UNCOMBED HAIR

When I see any of my grandchildren with their hair uncombed, it upsets me because I lived through an era when poor Black folks couldn't do any better. Now it seems to be a fad because I see people on the television doing it too. There were times when the only thing Black girls and women could do was tie a rag on their head because the hair was so matted and nappy that a comb couldn't be pushed through it. To me, this represents depression and oppression. I asked one of my granddaughters, "Why are you walking around here with your hair looking like that? Do you realize how you look?"

She said, "Grandma this is the style."

"Style! Style? No, it isn't." I know I'm old-fashioned and in the minority with the young folks of today, but I wish our young people wouldn't detract from themselves like that and comb their hair!

I CALL THEM RAGS

Who would've ever thought that people would be buying shredded up, raggedy, patched clothes? I see people wearing shirts and pants with holes all over them. They tell me the clothes are stylish and expensive. To me, it's just crazy. When I was a child, all we wore were holed and patched clothes because we couldn't do any better. I tell my grandchildren not to spend their money on clothes with holes, but to buy themselves some good quality, pretty clothes. It is incredible to me that what we once considered poor is now high fashion. Who would have thought?

I'M SORRY AND I FORGIVE

I'm an old lady, and I'm surprised to see so many adults that have a hard time saying they are sorry. Many people just don't know how to forgive. I believe the reason is that they didn't learn this as a child. If my children did something wrong, I would discipline them or talk in a way to make them feel ashamed for the wrong they'd done. If there was no shame, there was no sorrow.

They'd say they were sorry, and I'd say, "Alright I forgive you. Now don't do it again."

No one likes to always be reminded of what they've done wrong. The same is true for children. If you discipline your child once for an offense, don't keep bringing it up every time they do something else wrong. You're teaching them by your actions how NOT to forgive.

"Children are great imitators. So, give them something great to imitate."

Hopefully, you've enjoyed our compilations and gathered at least one "nugget" or "pearl" to enhance your life, as much as we've enjoyed sharing!

KINGDOM FRUIT

"I want to be able to bring forth fruit fit for God's kingdom." -Charity

One day, when pregnant with my first child, I was at my father's house. One of his sisters was visiting as well. She was a widow and a missionary in the church. She wanted children and unfortunately, couldn't have any. She was talking to my father about Hannah. She had read about Hannah in the Bible. She was sharing the story that Hannah went to the Lord and talked to him about having a child. Hannah had tried for so long and had not been able to conceive. She asked the Lord to bless her where she would be able to bring forth a son. If he did, she would give him back to the Lord.

There I was, pregnant and sitting in the next room, listening to their conversation. I had been praying for months that I wouldn't die when I had the baby. Remember, my mother died in childbirth, so this fear was real for me. After my aunt went home, the Lord gave me these words:

"Lord strengthen and able me to bring forth fruit fit for your kingdom. Bless me to have a missionary; let me be a missionary. If you give me this, I will give the baby back to you."

I didn't tell anyone about my prayer. I didn't only pray the prayer during that pregnancy, I prayed it every time I was pregnant. I tried to live what I prayed. God heard me and answered my prayers. I was blessed with eight beautiful and healthy children, four boys and four girls (Jorene, Ruth, Perry, LC, James, Lois, Willie and Berlinda).

I taught them to respect me and to obey. I also taught them to laugh and play, to have fun. As long as we were together, we were happy. I was blessed and honored to have fruit from my family tree, my eight gifts from God. I meant those words that I prayed on that day. I gave each one of them back to God and God answered my prayer. I had two missionaries, one pastor, one assistant pastor, two deacons, and six choir members within my eight children.

All of them are faithful to God, the church, and their families. They are my KINGDOM FRUIT. I now pray for every generation to come. I have five generations of fruit living in my family to continue my prayer for the kingdom.

"Now also when I am old and gray-headed, O God, forsake me not; until I have shewed thy strength unto this generation, and thy power to everyone that is to come." (Psalm 71:18 KJV)

Favorite Song:

> After the cloud rolled by
> After the last long sigh
> Praising Jehovah
> By the crystal sea
> There will be joy, yes there will be joy
> Throughout the ages, trouble, and ages
> After the cares, troubles, and cares
> Through a long life and over
> When we have reached, yes when we have reached
> That land of Beulah, land of Beulah
> There will be joy, yes there will be joy
> Forevermore!
>
> *— Author unknown*

Reflection Question:

What is your prayer for your family and generations to come?

ABOUT THE AUTHOR

As a dynamic speaker and strategic thought partner, Joy has delivered keynotes and workshops in more than twenty countries and across five continents. With more than twenty years of leadership experience across both nonprofit and for-profit business sectors, she is a highly sought executive coach skilled at helping leaders go from where they are, to where they aspire to be. Joy has served on boards for several organizations and was named by Diversity Journal as a "Woman Worth Watching," by Healthcare Businesswomen's Association as a "Rising Star," and by Black Enterprise as a Top Executive in Corporate Diversity.

A global leader in talent management, Joy has dedicated her career to improving the lives of individuals, one person at a time. Known as an inspirational leader, Joy has a rare ability to tackle very difficult subjects and speak truth to power without stirring negative emotions. She is skillful and experienced in developing business solutions that address people challenges to create a more diverse and inclusive work environment.

A leader in diversity and inclusion, Joy is an advocate and powerful voice in creating change for diverse populations. She seeks to create a world in which all people are treated with dignity and respect. She works tirelessly to champion inclusion by creating safe spaces for brave conversations on topics of injustice and inequities.

Joy currently serves as the Chief Diversity Officer of a Fortune 200 pharmaceutical company where she partners with Human Resources and business leaders to attract and develop talent, build future leaders at all levels, and improve diversity and inclusion across the company. Joy earned a Master's degree in strategic leadership and a Bachelor's degree in organizational development from the University of Memphis.

Joy is a devoted mother and wife. She is married to her college sweetheart, Tyron, and has two wonderful young adult children, Taylor and Tyron Jr.